QUESTIONS
AND ANSWERS ON

American
Citizenship

NEW REVISED EDITION

QUESTIONS
AND ANSWERS ON

American
Citizenship

SOLOMON WIENER

Eugene Goldstein, Legal Consultant
Newman, Aronson & Newman, P.C.

Regents Publishing Company, Inc.

The information given in this book is of a general nature and the immigration laws of the United States are under almost constant revision. The reader should consult an informed attorney for timely advice about specific situations.

ACKNOWLEDGMENTS

The author and publisher wish to express their appreciation to the following:

Elias Lieberman, for permission to use the poem "I Am An American," copyright 1918, 1946.

Irving Berlin Music Corporation, for permission to reprint the lyrics of the song "God Bless America."

E. P. Dutton & Co., Inc. for the use of the poem "America the Beautiful" by Katharine Lee Bates, from Poems.

Charles Scribner's Sons, for the use of the poem "America For Me" by Henry van Dyke, from The Poems of Henry van Dyke, copyright 1911 Charles Scribner's Sons; renewal copyright 1931 Tertiur van Dyke.

The Mastai Collection, for use of the historical flags on chapter-opening pages.

CREDITS

Cover Design: Kiffi Diamond
Cover Illustration by Jane Sterrett
Interior Design: Suzanne Bennett & Associates
Drawings: Erasmo Hernandez
Revision Coordinator: David A. Tillyer
Photo Research: Monique Peyrat, Milton Kaplan

Published by
Regents Publishing Company, Inc.
Two Park Avenue
New York, N.Y. 10016

Printed in the United States of America
ISBN 0-88345-485-8
10 9 8 7 6 5 4 3 2 1

Preface

This is a book for everybody—native-born citizens, naturalized citizens and future citizens—interested in becoming well-informed and responsible United States citizens.

It presents a clear, factual picture of the United States under such headings as:

American History (outstanding events and personalities)
National, state and local government
Documents of American Freedom
American Patriotic Literature
Miscellaneous Information

and then gives complete, authoritative and up-to-date information on Immigration and Naturalization, including most official forms in general use. The final section consists of Review Questions followed by Key Answers that can serve as aids to self-testing and self-checking the knowledge acquired from the text.

Apart from those who are citizens by birth and those who have become citizens through naturalization, there are many who look to the United States as a land of hope and opportunity. These are our future citizens who want to become worthy members of that community of more than 225 million men, women, and children that make up the United States of America. They want to participate in our democratic process, assume the duties and responsibilities of citizenship, pursue its ideals, and benefit from its privileges. This book can, through the essential information it offers, serve as their guide to attaining active, responsible citizenship.

It is hoped that this book will give the reader a deeper understanding of the American way of life and a greater sense of being a vital part of a nation that believes in the dignity and worth of the individual.

To the many persons who offered invaluable suggestions, I wish to express my thanks and appreciation. To my wife, I express my gratitude for her encouragement and assistance.

I wish particularly to acknowledge my gratitude to the Immigration and Naturalization Service, United States Department of Justice, for making available the most recent information on immigration and naturalization. Persons in need of guidance on any immigration or naturalization problem are urged to seek the assistance of this agency of the federal government.

I would like to dedicate this small effort to my daughters, Marjorie Diane and Willa Kay—grandchildren of immigrants.

New York, New York   Solomon Wiener

The Flag Of
The United States

The American Flag, in its present form, is well known around the world. Its symbolism is simple: Fifty white stars represent the fifty states of the Union, while the thirteen stripes are a permanent symbol of the original thirteen states. It is generally assumed that the only change the flag has undergone since the early days of the Republic is the addition of one state for each new state.

But in fact Congress made no specifications other than the essential elements (the stars and the stripes, and their respective colors) in its June 14, 1777, *Flag Resolution*. As a result, from the outset, Americans interpreted these indications as they saw fit. Thus, they created personal, highly imaginative, and often very beautiful versions of the national emblem. In addition to its patriotic significance therefore, the development of the design of the American Flag was a major manifestation of American folk-art, and as such constitutes an essential part of our cultural history.

Throughout the two centuries of its history, the flag of the United States has been called by many titles, of which the most famous are "The Stars and Stripes," "The Star-Spangled Banner" (a quotation from the national anthem) and "Old Glory." We should not forget, however, that it has also been hailed as "The Flag of the Free," "The Banner of Freedom," and "The People's Flag"—and that it deserves these names not only symbolically but also in the literal sense of its unhampered freedom of design.

The ten examples in this book are surviving period flags of unique design, each made for one individual owner and never duplicated. They furnish a bird's eye view of the progression of the United States flag through various periods in the country's history.

Boleslaw and Marie-Louise d'Otrange Mastai (authors of *The Stars and The Stripes: The American Flag as Art and as History from the Birth of the Republic to the Present*, Alfred Knopf, N.Y. 1973)

Contents

Citizenship

The Prisoners' Flag of thirteen stars, made by a seaman from an American ship captured during the Revolutionary period, and imprisoned in Devon, England. Circa 1780.

Who are the American people?

All the people of the United States are immigrants or the descendants of immigrants who settled in this country. Even the American Indians who were the original inhabitants of North America were immigrants—it is believed that they migrated from Asia.

How large is the United States?

It is almost as large as all of Europe. With a land area of approximately 3½ million square miles, it is the fourth largest country in the world.

What is the population of the United States?

There are more than 225 million people living in the United States.

Are all citizens of the United States native-born Americans?

No, U.S. citizens may be citizens either by birth or by naturalization.

What is meant by naturalization?

Naturalization is the legal process by which an alien becomes a U.S. citizen.

What is an alien?

An alien is a person who is not a citizen of the country in which he or she lives.

Are aliens living in the United States required to become American citizens?

No, legally admitted immigrants may remain in the United States without becoming American citizens.

What is an immigrant?

An immigrant is a person who leaves his or her native land to live in another country. For example, people who leave their native country and settle in the United States are immigrants.

Have many immigrants come to the United States since the Revolutionary War?

Yes. Since the American Revolutionary War, approximately 50 million immigrants have come to the United States.

Have many of these immigrants become naturalized citizens?

Yes. The process by which immigrants become naturalized citizens has been continuous since our country's beginning. From 1900 to the present time, more than 10 million aliens have become naturalized U.S. citizens.

Can persons of any race become naturalized citizens?

Yes, persons of any race can become naturalized citizens of the United States.

Why has the United States been called a "melting pot"?

Immigrants who settled in this country came from Europe, Africa, Latin America, the Middle East, Asia—from all parts of the world. According to the "melting pot" idea, all the customs and traditions of different races, religions, language groups and ethnic backgrounds blend into a new, unique way of life.

What is meant by Americanization?

Americanization means becoming familiar with, accepting and supporting the American way of life. It involves learning the language, customs and traditions of the United States, knowing its history, understanding the principles and form of its government, and appreciating its heritage. It means becoming a well-informed, loyal and responsible U.S. citizen.

What are the advantages of U.S. citizenship?

There are many advantages, including the privilege of being able to vote and thereby have a voice in government; the opportunity to work for government if you wish to do so, or to run for public office; and the protection of the United States while traveling abroad. In addition, certain professions, trades, and businesses require that their licensees be citizens.

Is the protection of law that Americans enjoy guaranteed to citizens only?

No. It applies to all people, citizens and non-citizens, living in the United States.

What are the duties and responsibilities of American citizenship?

Some of the duties and responsibilities of citizenship are:

to keep informed
to vote intelligently
to obey the laws
to support elected leaders
to pay taxes
to respect the rights of others
to serve on juries
to practice religious tolerance
to respect the opinions of others
to meet financial obligations
to protect the United States

In a democracy such as ours, how do people attempt to achieve political and social changes?

In a democracy such as ours, political and social changes are achieved by legislation. People attempt to influence our lawmakers by means of the ballot, through political parties and pressure groups, and by the use of mass media such as books, newspapers, magazines, radio, and television.

Are all U.S. citizens required to vote?

No, voting is not compulsory in the United States.

Do all citizens have the right to vote?

No. In order to vote, citizens must meet certain age and residence requirements.

What is the minimum voting age?

The minimum voting age in all federal, state, and local elections is 18 years.

Are voters required to belong to political parties?

No, voters are not required to join political parties.

What is meant by a polling place?

A polling place is a place where voters go to cast their ballots on election day.

Are the ballots cast by voters secret?

Yes, voting in the United States is by secret ballot.

What is a polling booth?

A polling booth is an enclosed compartment in which a citizen votes either on a voting machine or by paper ballot.

When is Election Day?

In almost all states, Election Day is the first Tuesday after the first Monday in November.

Voting machines were first used in the U.S. in 1894 in New York City. Some type of machine voting process is now used in all fifty states.

The L'Enfant Flag of thirteen stars set in the graceful oval pattern created for the Society of the Cincinnati by the celebrated major Pierre L'Enfant, designer of the City of Washington. The stars are not white but instead painted in gold. Circa 1783.

Who discovered America?

Christopher Columbus, an Italian navigator, discovered America in 1492 during an expedition financed by Queen Isabella of Spain.

How did America get its name?

Amerigo Vespucci, an Italian explorer, claimed that he had discovered a new continent. The continent was called America by geographers because of this claim. Actually, Vespucci explored the coast of South America five years after Columbus had discovered the new continent. However, Columbus was not aware of his own discovery; he believed, instead, that he had found a new route to India.

Who was the first Englishman to explore America?

John Cabot was commissioned by King Henry VII of England to discover new lands. In his explorations during 1497 and 1498, he sailed along the east coast of what is now the United States and claimed it for England.

What were the early settlers called?

The early settlers were called *colonists*. Their settlements were called *colonies*.

This Currier & Ives print of the landing of Columbus in the New World was made in 1892.

Who lived in America before the arrival of the settlers?

The inhabitants were called *Indians*, so named because of the belief that Columbus had found a new route to India.

From what countries did the first American settlers come?

The first immigrants to settle in this country came from various European countries. However, since most of the permanent settlers were English, the English language became the language of the newly discovered North America.

Where was the first permanent English settlement in America established?

The English established their first permanent settlement in Virginia in 1607. They named it Jamestown, in honor of King James of England.

Who were the Pilgrims?

The Pilgrims were a small group of people who came to America seeking religious freedom. They sailed from England on the *Mayflower* and established the second permanent English settlement at Plymouth, Massachusetts in 1620.

What was the Mayflower Compact?

The Mayflower Compact was the first plan of democratic government in America. It was drawn up by the Pilgrims aboard the *Mayflower*.

Why did the creation of the Virginia House of Burgesses represent an important step toward self-government?

In 1619, the Virginia colony obtained from England the right to elect representatives to a House of Burgesses. This body, with power to help make laws for the colony, was the first representative legislature in the Americas.

What famous English document was the basis for many American liberties?

The Magna Charta, signed by King John of England in 1215, recognized the rights of the people. It was one of the first important documents of political freedom.

This is an 1876 Currier & Ives print of the Pilgrims landing at Plymouth, Mass., on December 20, 1620.

How was the colony of Rhode Island founded?

Roger Williams, a Puritan preacher, objected to the requirement that all settlers attend the Puritan Church. He was forced by the Puritan leaders to leave Massachusetts in 1636. Roger Williams made his new home in Providence and founded the colony of Rhode Island where people could belong to any church.

Why was the founding of Rhode Island important?

It helped establish the basic democratic principle of religious freedom.

Which is the oldest college in the United States?

The Harvard College, established at Cambridge, Massachusetts, in 1636, is the oldest college in the United States.

What was the Toleration Act?

In 1649, the colony of Maryland, a Catholic settlement, passed the Toleration Act. It gave freedom of worship to all Christian settlers, regardless of the church to which they belonged.

Who ruled this country prior to 1775?

Great Britain ruled this country until 1775. The governors and other high officials were appointed by the King of England.

How did England attempt to raise money in the colonies?

The English Parliament passed laws imposing taxes which the colonists were required to pay. The tax on tea was among the longest held and most bitterly resented of the taxes.

Why did the colonists object to such tax laws?

The colonists objected because they felt that they were not represented in the English Parliament where such laws were passed. They believed that taxation without representation was unfair.

What was the Boston Tea Party?

The Boston Tea Party took place in 1773. Patriots, dressed as Indians, boarded ships loaded with tea from England and threw the tea into the water to show their dissatisfaction.

What was the First Continental Congress?

The First Continental Congress was a meeting of representatives from various colonies to express anger about British treatment of the colonists. The Congress met in Philadelphia in 1774.

The Battle of Lexington was the opening engagement of the American Revolutionary War.

When did the fighting between the colonists and England begin?

On April 19, 1775, fighting broke out between the colonists and English soldiers at Lexington and Concord in Massachusetts.

What was the Second Continental Congress?

The Second Continental Congress met in 1775 after the fighting had begun. This Congress conducted the war and made the final peace.

Who wrote the Declaration of Independence?

The Declaration of Independence was written by Thomas Jefferson. He later became the third president of the United States.

When was the Declaration of Independence adopted?

The Declaration of Independence was adopted officially by the Second Continental Congress on July 4, 1776, a little more than a year after the Revolutionary War had begun.

When was the title *The United States of America* first used officially?

This 1876 Currier & Ives print depicts the committee which composed the Declaration of Independence. They are (from the left) Thomas Jefferson, Roger Sherman, Benjamin Franklin, Robert R. Livingston, and John Adams.

The first offical use of this title occurred in the Declaration of Independence in 1776.

What does the Declaration of Independence contain?

The Declaration of Independence states the basic belief that all men are created equal and have been given the right of life, liberty, and the pursuit of happiness. It says that governments are established to protect these rights and derive their just powers from the consent of the governed. If any form of government tries to take away these rights, the people are free to change or abolish it and to set up a new form of government.

Twenty-seven specific charges against the English king, who deprived the colonists of their natural rights, are then listed, and the political ties between the colonies and Great Britain are declared broken. Finally, the birth of a new American nation is proclaimed.

What was this country's first war against England called?

The first war against England was called the Revolutionary War or the War of Independence. It began in 1775 and ended in 1783.

Did soldiers from other countries help the United States in its fight for independence?

Yes, soldiers from many European countries assisted the Americans —Lafayette of France, Kosciusko of Poland, Von Steuben from Prussia, De Kalb from Bavaria, and many others.

What was the plan of government before the adoption of the Constitution?

The thirteen states were governed by the Articles of Confederation.

What were some of the weaknesses of the Articles of Confederation?

Congress did not have the power to collect taxes; there was no chief executive to enforce the laws, and there were no courts to interpret the laws or protect the rights of the people.

What was done to remedy this situation?

A Constitutional Convention was called in 1787 to revise the Articles of Confederation. It decided that the government should be built upon a completely new plan and therefore drew up the *Constitution of the United States.*

Did the Constitution go into effect in 1787?

No, it went into effect on March 4, 1789, and a new government was formed.

What famous general of the Revolutionary War became the first president of the United States?

George Washington was the famous general who, after the war, became the first president of the United States.

Was the first capital of the United States located in Washington, D.C.?

No, the first capital of the United States was located in New York.

What famous patriot is known as the "Father of Our Country"?

George Washington is known as the "Father of Our Country" because of his role as commander in chief of the army during the Revolutionary War, his efforts in forming a new government, and his service as the first president of the United States.

For how long did George Washington serve as president?

He served as president for two terms (1789-1797). His refusal to run for a third term established the custom that no president should serve more than two terms.

Was this two-term tradition ever broken?

Yes, this tradition was broken only once, when President Franklin

George Washington and the Marquis de Lafayette are shown visiting soldiers at Valley Forge during the winter of 1777.

D. Roosevelt was elected to a third term in 1940. He was also elected to a fourth term in 1944.

How was the Louisiana Territory acquired by the United States?

The Louisiana Territory was purchased from France in 1803.

What was the name of the second war the United States fought with England?

The second war with England was known as the War of 1812.

What caused the War of 1812?

It came about because of England's disregard for American rights on the seas. England tried to stop American trade with France and removed sailors from U.S. ships.

When did the War of 1812 end?

A peace treaty was signed in 1814, and the United States gained commercial freedom of the seas.

What patriotic song was written during the War of 1812?

"The Star-Spangled Banner" was written by Francis Scott Key in 1814. He was inspired by the sight of the American flag still flying over Fort McHenry in Baltimore after an all-night enemy attack. It became the national anthem by Act of Congress in 1931.

Francis Scott Key observes all-night bombardment from aboard ship.

How was Florida acquired by the United States?
Florida was purchased from Spain in 1819.

What is the Monroe Doctrine?
In 1823, President James Monroe sent a message to Congress stating that North and South America were not open to further colonization by European powers; that European powers must not interfere in American affairs, and that the United States would not interfere in European affairs. This message has become known as the Monroe Doctrine.

What were the principal causes of the Civil War?
The split between the northern and southern states over the moral question of slavery, their different economic interests, and the legal question of the right to secede from the United States were the principal causes of the Civil War. It began when eleven southern states tried to secede from the United States. These southern states believed that slavery was commercially necessary and were afraid that the national government would legislate slavery out of existence. Fighting began with the attack by the southern states on Fort Sumter, a federal fort located in South Carolina.

When was slavery introduced into America?
Negro slaves were first brought to Virginia in 1619. Slavery spread to all the colonies but was concentrated to a large extent in the South.

When was the Civil War fought?
The Civil War began in 1861 and ended in 1865.

What was the Confederate States of America?
The Confederate States of America was the name of the government which the southern states formed after they seceded from the Union.

Who was chosen president of the Confederacy?
Jefferson Davis was elected president of the Confederate States of America in 1861.

What was the outcome of the Civil War?
The northern states won, slavery was abolished, and the Union was preserved. It established the principle that no state had the right to secede from the United States.

Who was Abraham Lincoln?
Abraham Lincoln was president of the United States during the Civil War.

This photograph of President Lincoln visiting Gen. George B. McClellan in the General's tent in Antietam, Md., was taken by Alexander Gardner in 1862.

What was the Emancipation Proclamation?

The Emancipation Proclamation, issued by Abraham Lincoln in 1863, freed the slaves in the rebelling states.

Did the Emancipation Proclamation abolish slavery everywhere in the United States?

No. It did not abolish slavery in those states that were not in rebellion.

When was slavery finally abolished?

The 13th Amendment, adopted in 1865, abolished slavery in the United States.

Who were the famous generals of the northern armies during the Civil War?

General Ulysses S. Grant and General William T. Sherman were the leaders of the northern forces during the Civil War. General Grant later became president of the United States (1869-1877).

General Robert E. Lee surrendered to General Ulysses S. Grant at Appomattox, Va.

Who were the famous generals of the southern armies during the Civil War?

General Robert E. Lee and General Thomas J. (Stonewall) Jackson were famous leaders of the southern forces during the Civil War. General Jackson died in battle during the Civil War.

What speech delivered by President Lincoln at the dedication of a national cemetery became a famous document of American history?

The Gettysburg Address, delivered by President Lincoln at the dedication of the battlefield of Gettysburg, Pennsylvania, as a national cemetery, has become an important document of American history. In it, Lincoln not only paid homage to the soldiers of the North and South who had died on the battlefield, but reaffirmed in a simple and sincere manner the democratic ideals of American government. (Text appears on page 187.)

How was Alaska acquired by the United States?

Alaska was purchased from Russia in 1867.

How was the Statue of Liberty acquired by the United States?

It was presented to the United States by the French government in 1886 to commemorate the alliance between the two countries during the American Revolution and their continuing friendship. The Statue of Liberty is located on Liberty Island in New York harbor.

What important trade union was formed in 1886?

The American Federation of Labor (A.F.L.) was formed in 1886.

When did the United States enter World War I?

The United States entered World War I on April 6, 1917.

What noted American military leader served in World War I?

General John J. Pershing commanded the American Expeditionary Forces (A.E.F.) in World War I.

When did World War I end?

World War I ended on November 11, 1918. This day was set aside originally as Armistice Day. It is now recognized as Veterans' Day.

Who was Woodrow Wilson?

Woodrow Wilson was president of the United States during World War I.

What famous American was the first to fly alone across the Atlantic Ocean?

Charles A. Lindbergh made the first one-man, non-stop flight across the Atlantic Ocean in 1927.

What is the Social Security Act?

The Social Security Act, signed by President Franklin D. Roosevelt in 1935, established old-age benefits and unemployment insurance.

What is the Fair Labor Standards Act?

The Fair Labor Standards Act, signed by President Roosevelt in 1938, provided for a minimum wage and a 40-hour work week.

What important labor union was formed in 1938?

The Congress of Industrial Organizations (C.I.O.) was formed in 1938.

When did World War II begin?

World War II began in 1939 when Germany invaded Poland.

When did the United States enter World War II?

The United States entered the war on December 8, 1941.

What prompted the United States to declare war on Japan?

On December 7, 1941, Japanese forces attacked Pearl Harbor, an American naval base in the Pacific. The following day, the United States declared war on Japan.

Who was president of the United States during World War II?

Franklin D. Roosevelt was president until April 12, 1945, the date of his death. Harry S Truman, his vice-president, succeeded him as president.

What statement made by President Roosevelt in 1941 to all Americans, as well as to the rest of the world, is considered a famous document of American history?

The "Four Freedoms" was contained in the president's annual message to Congress on January 6, 1941. It was regarded as a concise statement of the ideals for which Americans were prepared to fight.

President Roosevelt is shown here with Winston Churchill and Joseph Stalin at Yalta Conference at the end of World War II.

What were the four human freedoms in this message?

The four essential human freedoms expressed in this message were:

freedom of speech
freedom of worship
freedom from want
freedom from fear

Which noted American military leaders served in Europe during World War II?

General Dwight D. Eisenhower was supreme commander, Allied Forces. General Omar N. Bradley and General George S. Patton, Jr. served under him. General Eisenhower later became the 34th president of the United States.

Which noted American military leaders served in the Pacific during World War II?

General Douglas MacArthur was supreme commander in the Pacific; Admiral Chester W. Nimitz commanded the Pacific Fleet.

What is meant by V-E Day?

V-E (Victory in Europe) Day is the day Germany surrendered the war unconditionally—May 7, 1945.

Which two cities in Japan were destroyed by atomic bombs during World War II?

Hiroshima and Nagasaki were destroyed by atomic bombs in August 1945.

What is V-J Day?

V-J Day (September 2, 1945) is the day Japan signed the surrender terms of the war aboard the battleship *Missouri*.

How did World War II differ from previous wars fought by the United States?

World War II was a global war. It required the total effort of both the civilian and the military forces. The war, fought all over the world, was the most costly and destructive in the history of mankind.

What international organization was established in 1945?

The United Nations was officially established on October 24, 1945. Originally, there were 51 member nations. U.N. membership now exceeds 150 nations.

The United Nations General Assembly.

Where is the U.N. headquarters located?
> The United Nations headquarters is in New York City.

What action by North Korea resulted in armed intervention by the United States and other members of the United Nations?
> On June 25, 1950, North Korean forces crossed the 38th parallel and invaded South Korea. The United States and other members of the United Nations intervened on the side of South Korea.

When did the Korean conflict end?
> This conflict ended on July 27, 1953, when an armistice was signed.

What important labor merger took place in 1955?
> The A.F.L. and the C.I.O. combined in 1955 to form the A.F.L.-C.I.O., a labor union with more than 15 million members.

Who was the youngest person ever elected president of the United States?
> John F. Kennedy was the youngest person ever elected president. He was 43 years old when he was elected in 1960.*

Did President Kennedy serve a full term of office?
> No, he was assassinated on November 22, 1963, and was succeeded by Vice-President Lyndon B. Johnson.

Who was the only president of the United States to resign from office?
> President Richard M. Nixon resigned from office on August 9, 1974, rather than face impeachment by the House of Representatives on charges of obstructing justice in the Watergate case, refusing to comply with subpoenas and abusing his powers of office.

Who was the only president not elected to office?
> Gerald Ford was appointed vice-president by President Nixon, with Congressional approval, upon the resignation of Vice-President Spiro T. Agnew on October 10, 1973. Mr. Ford became president when Mr. Nixon resigned from the presidency; he was never elected to this office.

Who was the first American to travel in outer space?
> Alan B. Shepard, Jr., was lifted 115 miles into space on May 5, 1961. He was safely recovered by a helicopter after his ship landed in the Atlantic Ocean, 300 miles away from the launch site.

---

* Theodore Roosevelt was reelected vice-president of the United States in 1900 and succeeded to the presidency at age 42 upon the death of President William McKinley.

Edwin E. Aldrin, Jr., one of the first men to walk on the moon.

Who was the first American to orbit the earth?

John H. Glenn, Jr., first circled the globe on February 20, 1962. Since that time, other U.S. astronauts have orbited the earth. In 1974, Glenn was elected a United States Senator by the state of Ohio.

Have American astronauts ever landed on the moon?

Yes. On July 20, 1969, Neil A. Armstrong and Edwin E. Aldrin, Jr., landed on the moon, while Michael Collins continued orbiting the moon in the Apollo command ship. The following day, the two moon explorers rocketed away from the moon and linked up with the Apollo command ship. Four days later, all three astronauts were safely recovered after they splashed down in the Pacific Ocean. This feat has been repeated by other American astronauts.

What was the U.S. involvement in the Vietnam War?

In the long civil war between North Vietnam and South Vietnam, the U.S. initially furnished South Vietnam with military advisers and only token forces. This military support eventually escalated to more than half a million men in 1969. Most Americans opposed greater involvement in the Vietnam War, and on March 29, 1973, the last U.S. troops left and military aid ceased.

What is the role of the United States in world affairs?

The United States is a powerful nation that exercises great political and economic influence throughout the world. Many weaker nations seek the assistance of the United States in their fight against oppression and in their efforts to gain political freedom.

What are some of the economic problems facing the United States?

Some of the major economic problems of the United States are controlling inflation, providing employment for all people who are willing and able to work, and meeting the increasing demand for fuel. Other problems include the training of people for more responsible and skilled work; increasing productivity; the retraining of people whose jobs are threatened by advancing technology; and the conservation of energy.

What are some of the major social problems facing the United States?

Discrimination against minority groups is one of the most serious and difficult problems. Progress in helping to solve this problem is being made so that all Americans will enjoy full political, civil, and human rights, regardless of race, color, creed, national origin, or sex. Another important problem involves making our large cities safer and more desirable places in which to live and work.

State
and Local
Government

The Minerva Flag of thirteen stars was flown on the Revolutionary privateer
MINERVA. The boldly patterned stars with blunted tips were designed for
easy visibility at sea. Circa 1780.

State Government

What are the major functions of state government?

The major functions of state government are:

to protect life and property
to guard the health of the people
to provide education
to care for those in need
to construct and maintain roads
to protect the state's resources
to regulate corporations, trades and professions

How does the state government obtain income to conduct its activities?

State revenue comes principally from taxes on income, sales taxes, taxes on gasoline, fees for auto licenses, etc.

Where is the capital of your state located?

The capital of my state is located in . . . .

Do states have three branches of government?

Yes, states have three branches of government—the legislative branch, the executive branch and the judicial branch.

Do the states have a system of "checks and balances" similar to that of the federal government?

Yes, each state has a system of "checks and balances" consisting of the governor, the state legislature and the state courts.

How many states are there in the United States?

There are 50 states in the United States.

What are the names of the two most-recently admitted states?

Alaska and Hawaii were admitted in 1959. Alaska became the 49th state; Hawaii became the 50th state.

What geographic characteristics distinguish the two newest states from the other states?

Neither Alaska nor Hawaii border on any other state. Alaska is separated from the 48 states by Canada and the Pacific Ocean. Hawaii is separated from North America by the Pacific Ocean, and lies 2000 miles southwest of San Francisco.

How can a new state be created?

A new state can be created only by Congress.

Can a state be sued by the federal government?
Yes, it can be sued in the United States Supreme Court.

Can a state be sued by another state?
Yes, it can be sued in the United States Supreme Court.

Which is the largest state in the United States?
Alaska is the largest state in the United States. It is more than twice as large as Texas.

What is the smallest state in the United States?
Rhode Island is the smallest state in the United States.

Who is the chief executive of the state?
The governor is the chief executive of the state.

What is the name of the governor of your state?
The name of the governor of my state is . . . .

How are governors chosen?
They are elected directly by the people of the state.

For how long are governors elected?
Their terms vary by state. They are usually elected for either two or four years.

Can the governor be removed during his term of office?
Yes, he may be impeached by the state legislature. If found guilty of charges, he is removed from office.

If the governor dies, who takes over his powers and duties?
The lieutenant-governor becomes governor of the state.

Who makes the state laws?
The state legislature makes the state laws.

How are members of the state legislature chosen?
They are elected directly by the people of the state.

Do state legislatures consist of two houses?
With the exception of Nebraska, the state legislatures consist of two houses. Nebraska's legislature consists of only one house.

What are these legislative houses called?
They are usually called the House of Representatives or the Assembly, and the Senate.

For how long are members of state legislatures elected?

Length of term varies by state. State senators are usually elected for either two or four years; members of the Assembly are usually elected for either one or two years.

How are state laws made?

The method is similar to that for federal laws. A bill is passed by the state legislature and then approved by the governor.

What is the highest law of the state?

The state constitution is the highest law of the state. However, the state constitution must not violate the federal constitution which is the highest law of the land.

What do state constitutions generally contain?

State constitutions generally contain—

a preamble setting forth the purpose of the state government;
a bill of rights of the people;
a statement of the organization and powers of the state government;
rules for conducting elections;
rules for amending the constitution.

Does each state have its own constitution?

Yes, each state has its own constitution.

Can the state constitution be changed?

Yes, amendments to the state constitution may be proposed by the state legislature or at a state convention. They must then be ratified by the people of the state.

What does the judicial branch consist of?

The judicial branch consists of the state courts. Some state courts deal with criminal cases, others deal with civil cases. Decisions of lower courts may be appealed by taking such cases to the higher courts.

Local Government

What different kinds of local government are there within each state?

The different kinds of local government are those for governing counties, cities, towns, townships and special districts.

How do local governments obtain revenue to conduct their activities?

Local governments obtain money by means of taxes on property, the issuance of licenses, the collection of fees, etc. Some local governments have a sales tax and an income tax as well. Federal and state aid have also become important revenue sources.

What are counties?

Counties are major subdivisions of a state.

How many counties are there in the United States?

There are more than 3000 counties in the United States.

Are all states subdivided into counties?

No, counties exist in every state except Louisiana, Alaska, Rhode Island and Connecticut. Louisiana is divided into parishes which are the same as counties. Alaska, now divided into judicial districts, is planning to establish boroughs which will be similar to counties.

Which state has the greatest number of counties?

With 254 counties, Texas has the greatest number.

What are the major functions of city government?

The major functions of city government are:

to protect life and property
to provide health facilities
to provide education
to care for those in need
to provide recreational facilities
to make available adequate transportation

Do cities have constitutions?

No, they do not have constitutions. They receive charters from state legislatures. These charters describe the cities' organization and define their powers.

Do the cities have a system of "checks and balances" similar to that of the federal and state governments?

Yes, each city has a system of "checks and balances" consisting of the mayor or city manager, the city council and the municipal courts.

What forms of government organization are found in cities?

The principal forms of government organization found in cities are:

> mayor-council
> concil-manager
> commission

With the mayor-council form, the voters elect the mayor, other city officials and the city council. Although the council is the legislative body and determines policy, the mayor is the real administrative head.

With the council-manager form, the voters elect a small council who selects a city manager. The council has the policy-making power of the city but responsibility for administration rests with the city manager.

With the commission form, the city is governed by elected commissioners who individually serve as department heads and collectively constitute the legislative body.

Although the council-manager form of government is popular in small and medium-sized cities, it has not gained acceptance in the country's largest cities.

Which kind of local government—county, city, town, township or special district—is most numerous in the United States?

Special district governments exist in all 50 states and are the most numerous. There are more than 50,000 special districts, most of which are school districts. Other types of special districts are fire protection, soil conservation, water supply and drainage.

National Government

The Flag of Twenty Stars, believed to be the only surviving period flag of this number of stars. Flags of twenty stars were in use for little more than a year, from April 13, 1818 to July 4, 1819, when the twenty-first state, Illinois, called for an additional star.

What is a republic?
A republic is a form of government in which the people rule through freely elected representatives and an elected chief executive who are responsible to the people.

What is a democracy?
A democracy is a form of government in which the supreme power is held by the people. The government is elected by and gets all its power from the people.

Is the United States form of government a republic or a democracy?
It is actually both a republic and a representative democracy.

What is meant by national government?
National government means government of the entire nation—the government of the United States of America.

What is meant by federal government?
Federal government is the same as national government. It is so called because the United States is a federation or union of many states.

Who are the rulers in the United States?
The people have the actual power and authority to rule.

How do the people rule?
The people rule through their chosen representatives. Officials are either elected by the people or appointed by those who have been elected by the people.

What are the colors of the flag of the United States of America?
The colors of the flag of the United States are red, white and blue.

How many stars and stripes does the flag of the United States have?
The flag has 50 stars and 13 stripes.

What other expressions are used in referring to the American flag?
The flag of the United States is also called "Stars and Stripes," "Star-Spangled Banner," and "Old Glory."

Does the design of the American flag have any significance?

Yes. The seven red and six white stripes represent the original thirteen states; the blue field with fifty stars represents the Union of fifty states. The following quotation is attributed to George Washington who helped to design the flag:

"We take the stars from heaven, the red from our mother country, separating it by white stripes, thus showing that we have separated her, and the white stripes shall go down to posterity representing liberty."

What is the Liberty Bell?

The Liberty Bell is associated with the historic events of the War of Independence. It hangs in Independence Hall in Philadelphia where the Declaration of Independence was adopted on July 4, 1776.

What does the Liberty Bell symbolize?

It symbolizes the freedoms, as well as the rights, privileges, and opportunities, of all Americans.

What is the Great Seal of the United States of America?

The Great Seal was adopted by the Continental Congress in 1782 and by the federal government in 1789 as a national symbol.

Does the design of the Great Seal have any significance?

Yes. On the front side, the seven white and six red stripes on the shield represent the thirteen original states. The North American bald eagle holds an olive branch in its right talon and a bundle of thirteen arrows in its left talon to show that this country prefers peace but is prepared to fight. On the scroll in the eagle's beak is inscribed *E Pluribus Unum* which means "One from Many"—one nation made up of many states. The thirteen stars over the eagle's head are in a field surrounded by clouds and symbolize the birth of a new nation.

The reverse side of the seal shows an incomplete pyramid of thirteen steps above which is a burst of light with an eye inside a triangle, symbolizing "The Eternal Eye of God." The words *Annuit Coeptis* over the eye means "God has favored our undertaking." The Roman numerals MDCCLXXVI on the base of the pyramid represents 1776. The motto *Novus Ordo Seclorum* stands for "A New Order of the Ages."

Where can the Great Seal be seen?

Both sides of the Great Seal are shown on the reverse side of every one-dollar bill.

Is Uncle Sam an official symbol of the United States?

No. Uncle Sam is a nickname which was first used during the War of 1812 to represent the United States government and people. Uncle Sam has been popularized in cartoons as a tall, thin man with a long, narrow beard, wearing a high hat and a long-tailed coat.

What is the official motto of the United States?

The national motto, officially adopted in 1956, is "In God We Trust."

Why was the American bald eagle chosen as the emblem of the United States?

The Continental Congress selected this eagle as a national emblem because it is native to North America. It symbolizes strength, vigilance and courage.

What is the national anthem of the United States?

"The Star-Spangled Banner" is the national anthem.

How is revenue obtained to conduct governmental activities?

Revenue, or money to pay for government services, is obtained largely by taxation.

What are some of the taxes the national government imposes?

Most of the national income comes from individual and corporate income taxes, and social insurance taxes. Additional income is obtained from excise taxes and customs duties.

Are the salaries of government officials subject to income tax?

Yes. Government officials pay an income tax on their salaries.

What is meant by excise taxes and customs duties?

Excise taxes are taxes on the manufacture or sale of commodities within the country (cigarettes, gasoline, liquors, etc.). Customs duties are taxes on goods purchased abroad and brought into the country.

What is a political party?

A political party is an association of citizens who have similar beliefs regarding political and economic issues, both domestic and foreign.

What type of party system exists in the United States?

The United States has a two-party system, with two major political parties.

What are the two major political parties in the United States?

The two major political parties are the Democrats and the Republicans. The symbol of the Democratic party is a donkey; the symbol of the Republican party is an elephant.

What other types of party systems are there?

The one-party system, in existence in the U.S.S.R., requires voting for candidates of the party in power. The multi-party system, in existence in France, permits a choice of candidates from many political parties.

The Democratic symbol (left) and the Republican symbol are seen in voting booths.

What is meant by voting a "straight party ticket?"
Voting for all candidates of one political party is called voting a "straight party ticket."

What is meant by voting a "split ticket?"
Voting for candidates from more than one political party is called voting a "split ticket."

Are there American political parties other than the Democratic and Republican parties?
Yes, there are other parties, such as the Conservatives, the Liberal party, the Libertarian party, the National States' Rights party, the Socialist Labor party, etc.

What are the three branches of the federal government?
The three branches of the federal government are the legislative branch, the executive branch and the judicial branch.

What is the function of each of these branches of government?
The legislative branch (Congress) makes the laws; the executive branch (President) carries out the laws; the judicial branch (Supreme Court) interprets the laws and judges violations.

What is meant by "separation of powers?"
"Separation of powers" means that the legislative, executive, and judicial functions are performed by different groups of people.

What is meant by a system of "checks and balances?"

A system of "checks and balances" is closely related to the principle of "separation of powers." By giving each branch of government partial power, the people prevent any one branch from becoming too powerful.

For example, a bill must be passed by both houses of Congress and approved by the president. If the president vetoes a bill, it may still become law if both houses of Congress override the veto by a two-thirds vote. The Supreme Court may, after review, declare the law unconstitutional and therefore invalid.

The Executive Branch

Who is the chief executive of the United States?

The president of the United States is the chief executive.

What is the name of the president of the United States?

The president of the United States is . . . .

For how many years is the president elected?

The president's term of office is four years.

When does the president take office?

The president takes office on the 20th day of January following his election.

Is an oath of office required before the president assumes his duties?

Yes, the Constitution requires that the president take an oath upon entering office.

What is the oath taken by the president?

The following oath is taken at the inauguration:

"I do solemnly swear (or affirm) that I will faithfully execute the office of president of the United States and will, to the best of my ability, preserve, protect and defend the Constitution of the United States."

Who administers the oath?

Any authorized officer could do so. However, it is customary for the chief justice of the United States to administer the oath.

When are presidential elections held?

Presidential elections are held every four years, for example— 1984, 1988, 1992, etc.

How are candidates for president and vice-president nominated?

Several months before Election Day, each political party nominates it candidates for president and vice-president at a national convention. Such conventions are held every four years.

Do the voters elect the president of the United States directly?

No, the people vote for electors who in turn elect the president and the vice-president.

How are the electors chosen?

Each state chooses a number of electors equal to the number of its senators plus its representatives in the House. It is customary for each elector to vote for the candidates of the political party that elected him to the electoral college.

What is the electoral college?

The electoral college consists of the electors who meet in their respective states to vote for president and vice-president.

What happens after the votes are cast?

The electoral votes are sent to the president of the Senate who counts them in the presence of both houses of Congress.

General Dwight D. Eisenhower was elected president in 1952 and reelected in 1956.

How many votes are needed by a candidate for election?

A successful candidate must obtain a majority of the votes of the electoral college.

What happens if no candidate receives a majority vote?

If no candidate for president receives a majority vote, the House of Representatives elects the president from among the three top candidates. However, each state has only one vote in such presidential selection.

If no candidate for vice-president receives a majority vote, the Senate elects the vice-president. Only the two top candidates are considered and a majority vote is required.

For how many terms may a person be elected to the office of president of the United States?

The 22nd Amendment, adopted in 1951, provides that no person may be elected for more than two terms.

What are the legal qualifications for the office of president of the United States?

One must be a native-born citizen, be at least 35 years old, and have resided in the United States for at least 14 years.

What are the duties of the president of the United States?

The president has many duties. Some of the more important ones are:

to see that the federal laws are enforced
to make treaties with other nations
to appoint important federal officials
to command the armed forces
to recommend measures to Congress
to approve or veto bills passed by Congress

President Ronald Reagan became the 40th president of the United States in 1981. Was he the 40th person to serve in that office?

No, only 39 persons have been president of the United States. Grover Cleveland served two separate terms as the 22nd and the 24th president.

Can foreign-born citizens of the United States ever become president of the United States?

No, foreign-born citizens of the United States can hold any office except that of president or vice-president of the United States.

May a child born in this country of parents who are aliens or naturalized citizens become president?
Yes, any native-born citizen may become president of the United States.

What is the president's residence called?
It is called the White House.

What is a presidential veto?
A veto is the power a president has to disapprove a bill even though it has been passed by both houses of Congress.

Has the president the right to declare war?
No, the right to declare war is reserved for Congress.

What is meant by the president's Cabinet?
The president's Cabinet consists of the heads of the thirteen executive departments and any other official whom the president may designate.

What is the purpose of the president's Cabinet?
The Cabinet advises the president and assists him in carrying out his duties as head of the executive branch of the national government.

What are the thirteen executive departments?
The thirteen executive departments are:

Department of State
Department of the Treasury
Department of Defense
Department of Justice
Department of the Interior
Department of Agriculture
Department of Commerce
Department of Labor
Department of Health and Human Services
Department of Housing and Urban Development
Department of Transportation
Department of Energy
Department of Education

What is the Council of Economic Advisers and what is its purpose?
The Council of Economic Advisers was established within the office of the president in 1946. The Council analyzes the national economy, advises the president on economic developments, evaluates the economic programs and policies of the federal government,

recommends to the president policies for economic growth and stability, and assists in the preparation of economic reports of the president to Congress.

What is the National Security Council?

The National Security Council was placed in the office of the president in 1949. The Council advises the president with respect to the integration of domestic, foreign, and military policies relating to national security.

What is the name of the most recently established executive department?

The most recently established executive department is the Department of Education.

What are the chief functions of the thirteen executive departments?

Their chief functions are:

Department of State—is concerned with foreign affairs

Department of the Treasury—manages the nation's financial affairs

Department of Defense—directs the army, navy and air force

Department of Justice—is the legal representative of the federal government and gives legal advice to other governmental agencies

Department of the Interior—is concerned with conserving the nation's natural resources

Department of Agriculture—is concerned with problems of the farmer and with improving plants, animals and soil

Department of Commerce—works to promote trade and commerce

Department of Labor—works to promote the welfare of labor

Department of Health and Human Services—is concerned with public health matters, the enforcement of food and drug laws, social security, and health care development

Department of Housing and Urban Development—is concerned with problems of housing, urban development and mass transportation

Department of Transportation—develops national policies and programs, and promotes the efficient utilization and conservation of the nation's resources

Department of Energy—provides the framework for a balanced national energy plan through the coordination and administration of the energy functions of the federal government

Department of Education—is concerned with matters such as elementary and secondary education, vocational and adult education, educational research and special education and rehabilitative services

Are Cabinet officers elected?

No, they are appointed by the president and approved by the Senate.

Is the attorney general in charge of any executive department?

Yes, the attorney general is the head of the Department of Justice.

Are there offices and establishments other than the thirteen regular departments in the executive branch?

Yes, there are approximately 55 independent agencies in the executive branch of the federal government.

What are the names of some of the more important independent agencies in the executive branch?

Some of the more important independent offices and establishments are:

Civil Aeronautics Board
Commission on Civil Rights
Equal Employment Opportunity Commission
Federal Communications Commission
Federal Deposit Insurance Corporation
Federal Trade Commission
General Services Administration
Interstate Commerce Commission
National Aeronautics and Space Administration
National Labor Relations Board
Office of Personnel Management
Selective Service System
Small Business Administration
Tennessee Valley Authority
United States Postal Service
Veterans' Administration

If the president dies, resigns or is incapacitated, who takes over his powers and duties?

The vice-president becomes president of the United States.

What is the order of succession to the presidency in the event that both the president and the vice-president die, resign or are unable to perform their duties?

The order of succession is as follows:

1. Speaker of the House of Representatives
2. President *pro tempore* of the Senate
3. Secretary of State
4. Secretary of the Treasury
5. Secretary of Defense
6. Attorney General
7. Secretary of the Interior
8. Secretary of Agriculture
9. Secretary of Commerce
10. Secretary of Labor
11. Secretary of Health and Human Services
12. Secretary of Housing and Urban Development
13. Secretary of Transportation
14. Secretary of Energy
15. Secretary of Education

When an official succeeds to the presidency based on the order of presidential succession, must the official meet any special requirement?

Yes, the official must meet the constitutional requirements for the presidency.

Can the president be removed during his term of office?

Yes, he may be impeached by Congress for treason, bribery, or any other serious crime. If found guilty, he is removed from office.

What is the meaning of "impeach?"

Impeach means to charge a public official with misconduct while in office.

Has any president ever been removed from office?

No. However, the attempt to remove Andrew Johnson, who was impeached in 1868, was defeated by only a single vote.

What is the name of the vice-president of the United States?

The vice-president's name is . . . .

Must the vice-president have the same qualifications for office as the president?

Yes, he must have the same qualifications.

For how many years is the vice-president elected?
> The vice-president's term of office is the same as that for the president—four years.

What are the duties of the vice-president?
> The duties of the vice-president, as provided in the Constitution, are—
>> to preside over the Senate;
>> to take over the office of the presidency in the event the president dies, resigns or is incapacitated.

Is the presiding officer of the Senate the same as the president *pro tempore* of the Senate?
> No, the vice-president of the United States is the presiding officer of the Senate. The president *pro tempore* is elected by the Senate from among its members and acts as presiding officer only during the absence of the vice-president.

Can the vice-president vote when he presides over the Senate?
> The vice-president can vote only when there is a tie vote in the Senate.

The Legislative Branch

What legislative bodies make up the Congress of the United States?
> Congress consists of two legislative bodies—the House of Representatives and the Senate.

What is meant by the "upper house" and the "lower house" of Congress?
> The Senate is known as the "upper house," and the House of Representatives is known as the "lower house."

When does Congress meet?
> Congress meets regularly once a year on January 3rd and remains in session until its members vote to adjourn.

What is meant by a *quorum*?
> In both the Senate and the House of Representatives, a majority of the membership constitutes a *quorum*. A *quorum* is needed in order to transact official business in either house.

Can the president of the United States call a special session of Congress?
> Yes, the president can call a special session of Congress whenever he thinks it necessary for Congress to act on an urgent matter.

Where does Congress meet?
Congress meets in Washington, D.C., the national capital.

Is there any difference between "Capital" and "Capitol?"
Yes, there is. The national capital is Washington, D.C. The United States Capitol is the building in which Congress meets.

Are visitors allowed to watch Congress is session?
Yes, both the Senate and the House of Representatives have visitors' galleries.

What is meant by a "congressman?"
Althought the term congressman refers to a member of either the Senate or the House of Representatives, it is generally used for a member of the House of Representatives. The official title for a member of the Senate is senator; for a member of the House of Representatives it is representative in Congress.

How are congressmen elected?
Representatives are elected by direct vote of the people who live in the same congressional district.

The United States Capitol

What are the legal qualifications for a representative?

A representative must be at least 25 years old, have been a citizen for at least seven years and be a resident of the state from which he is sent to Congress.

Who is the representative in Congress from your district?

The name of the representative from my congressional district is

. . . .

Does each state have the same number of representatives?

No, membership in the House of Representatives is apportioned among the states according to population. However, each state, regardless of population, must have at least one representative.

For how long are representatives elected?

Representatives are elected for two years.

Do all representatives have the same term of office?

Yes, the term of office for all representatives begins at the same time and expires at the end of the second year.

Does this mean that inexperienced representatives are elected every two years?

No, many of the representatives are reelected. These experienced lawmakers assist the newly elected members.

What is the difference between a term and a session of Congress?

A term of Congress begins on January 3rd of each odd-numbered year and lasts for two years. Each term is divided into two sessions. The first session of the term is the first year; the second session is the last year of the term.

What is the membership of the House of Representatives?

The membership of the House of Representatives is fixed by law at 435. With the admission of new states, the number is temporarily increased to give the new states representation. However, when reapportionment takes place, the number is reduced to 435 again.

Is there any special membership in the House of Representatives?

Yes. A Resident Commissioner from Puerto Rico and delegates from the District of Columbia, Guam and the Virgin Islands have the same rights and privileges as the other members except for the right to vote.

Who is the presiding officer of the House of Representatives?
The House of Representatives elects one of its members as the presiding officer. He is called the Speaker of the House.

What are the legal qualifications for a senator?
A senator must be at least 30 years old, have been a citizen for at least nine years and be a resident of the state from which he is sent to Congress.

Does the term "senior senator" refer to the age of a senator?
No, "senior" (or "junior") refers to a senator's length of service and not to his age.

Who are the two senators from your state?
The names of the two senators from my state are . . . . and . . . .

What is the membership of the Senate?
There are 100 members in the Senate.

Does each state, regardless of size or population, have the same number of senators?
Yes, there are two senators elected from each state.

For how long are senators elected?
Senators are elected for six years.

Does the term of office for all senators expire at the same time?
No, the term of office for one-third of the senators expires every two years. Accordingly, one-third of the senate is chosen every two years.

What is the advantage of electing only one-third of the Senate every two years?
The advantage is that after each election at least two-thirds of the senators are experienced, and they can assist the newly elected members.

Who presides over the Senate?
The vice-president of the United States presides over the Senate.

What are the duties of the president *pro tempore* of the Senate?
His duties are to preside over the Senate during the absence of the vice-president.

Can the president *pro tempore* vote in the Senate?

Yes, he can vote on all matters.

Is there any difference between a bill and an act?

Yes, a bill is a proposed law that has been introduced in the legislature. After the bill has been passed by both houses and then signed by the president, it becomes law and is referred to as an act.

What is meant by "lobbying?"

Lobbying refers to the efforts made by individuals or groups to influence legislators to vote for or against proposed legislation.

What is meant by the term "filibuster?"

Filibuster is the term used to describe delaying tactics used by lawmakers to prevent action on matters being considered by the legislative body.

How does a bill become a law?

1. A bill may be introduced in either house of Congress. However, revenue bills must originate in the House of Representatives.
2. If the bill is passed by a majority of both houses, it is sent to the president of the United States.
3. If the president of the United States approves and signs the bill, it becomes law.

Can a law be passed by Congress without the approval of the president of the United States?

Yes, if the president vetoes a bill, it is returned to Congress. The bill must then be passed by a two-thirds vote of both houses to become law without the president's signature or approval. Also, while Congress is in session, a bill becomes a law if it is not signed by the president within ten days.

Does either house of Congress have special powers?

Yes, the Senate alone can approve or disapprove major presidential appointments by majority vote, and it can ratify treaties made with foreign countries by a two-thirds vote. All bills concerned with the raising of money, such as taxes, duties, etc., must originate in the House of Representatives.

Are all congressmen required to study and analyze the thousands of bills introduced in Congress each year?

No, the matter of conducting hearings, studying and reporting on the thousands of proposed bills presented in Congress in handled by different committees.

How many committees are there in Congress?
There are 15 Standing Committees in the Senate and 22 Standing Committees in the House of Representatives.

What is the membership of these committees?
The Senate Standing Committees average about 15 members each. Senators are generally assigned to approximately eight different committees.

The Standing Committees of the House of Representatives average about 30 members each. All representatives receive at least one committee assignment.

Does Congress have its own official journal?
Yes, the *Congressional Record* is the official journal. It contains the daily proceedings of Congress.

Are there any federal offices or establishments directly responsible to Congress?
Yes, there are several such agencies, i.e., the Library of Congress, the Government Printing Office and the General Accounting Office.

The Judicial Branch

What are the functions of the judicial branch of the federal government?
It is the duty of the judicial branch of the national government—

to explain and interpret the laws;
to settle disputes between citizens of different states;
to try persons accused of violating federal laws;
to determine the constitutionality of laws.

Does the judicial branch of the federal government consist of only the Supreme Court?
No, it is made up of the Supreme Court and lower federal courts, such as the Courts of Appeals, the District Courts and other special courts.

What is the highest court in the United States?
The federal Supreme Court is the highest court of the land.

Can a decision of the United States Supreme Court be appealed to a higher body?
No, the decision of the Supreme Court is final. It cannot be overruled.

How many justices are there on the federal Supreme Court?

There are nine Supreme Court justices. One is the chief justice; the others are associate justices.

What is the name of the chief justice of the United States?

The chief justice of the United States is . . . .

Are the justices of the Supreme Court elected by the people?

No, they are appointed by the president of the United States. Such appointments must be confirmed by the Senate.

Are Supreme Court justices appointed for a certain number of years?

No, they are appointed for life.

What are the legal qualifications for a federal judge?

There are no legal qualifications for a federal judge. However, it is customary to appoint capable persons with legal training to federal judgeships.

Must the vote of the Supreme Court justices be unanimous in order to reach a decision?

No, only a majority vote is required. When all nine justices vote, a majority requires at least five votes.

Does the Supreme Court naturalize aliens?

No, the United States District Court, one of the lower federal courts, naturalizes aliens.

What is meant by a law being "unconstitutional?"

A law is unconstitutional when the federal Supreme Court finds that it violates the Constitution of the United States.

Can the president or Congress abolish the Supreme Court?

No, the Constitution established the Supreme Court. It can be abolished only by amendment to the Constitution of the United States.

What is the difference between a criminal case and a civil case?

A criminal case is one in which a person is tried for breaking a law. A civil case is one in which two parties disagree about their rights under the law.

About the Constitution

What is meant by the Articles of Confederation?

The Articles of Confederation was the plan of government prior to the adoption of the Constitution.

Why was the government under the Articles of Confederation unsatisfactory?

Under the Articles of Confederation, each state retained its full independence, and the central government had no real power.

What benefit was derived from the Articles of Confederation?

The Articles of Confederation enabled this nation to form a government based on a written document. Although the government under the Articles of Confederation was weak, it prepared the way for a stronger and more effective national government.

Who wrote the Constitution of the United States?

The Constitution was written by delegates from the different states who met in Philadelphia in 1787.

What name was given to those who favored ratification of the Constitution?

Those who favored ratification of the Constitution were called *Federalists*.

What was the major objection to the ratification of the Constitution?

Many patriots opposed ratification of the Constitution because it did not guarantee individual liberty.

What was done to satisfy those who originally opposed ratification of the Constitution?

A promise was made to add a Bill of Rights.

Were any individual rights included in the Constitution before the Bill of Rights was adopted?

Yes, there were several individual rights. However, people felt that additional rights were necessary to protect their freedom.

What is the Bill of Rights?

The Bill of Rights is the first ten amendments to the Constitution. It sets forth the individual's rights and liberties.

What are some of the rights and liberties guaranteed by the Bill of Rights?

Some of the more important rights and liberties are:

> freedom of religion, speech and the press
> right of assembly and petition
> right of due process of law
> right to a fair and speedy trial
> right to keep and bear arms
> the right not to have excessive fines or cruel and unusual punishment inflicted

Are the rights and freedoms guaranteed by the Bill of Rights for citizens only?

No, these rights and freedoms apply to all persons living in the United States.

What powers are reserved for the individual states?

The 10th Amendment states that the federal government has only those powers that have been delegated to it. All other powers belong to the individual state governments, as described in the individual state constitutions. They have control over such state and local matters as public health and safety, public welfare, education, marriage and divorce, transportation, etc.

Were other individual rights added to the Constitution after the Bill of Rights was adopted?

Yes, the following amendments added additional individual rights:

13th Amendment, adopted in 1865, abolished slavery

14th Amendment, adopted in 1868, gave citizenship to all persons born or naturalized in the United States

15th Amendment, adopted in 1870, prohibited states from taking away from male citizens the right to vote because of race, color or previous condition of servitude

19th Amendment, adopted in 1920, gave women the right to vote

26th Amendment, adopted in 1971, lowered the voting age to 18 years

Does this mean that women could not vote before 1920?

Yes, the right to vote was granted to women only after the adoption of the 19th Amendment in 1920.

Does this mean that 18-year-olds could not vote before 1971?

Yes. Before 1971, the minimum age requirement for voting in most states was 21 years. In only two states, Georgia and Kentucky, was the legal voting age set at 18 years. In Alaska, the legal voting age was 19 years; in Hawaii, 20 years.

Is there an overlapping of powers delegated to the national government and those reserved for the individual state governments?

Yes, there is an overlapping and a sharing of powers, especially in such areas as labor, social welfare and education.

Why is "States' Rights" a major political problem of American government?

The expansion of the federal government's activities into matters which were formerly local problems handled by the states has led to widespread differences of opinion and continued disagreement. One political group believes that such problems can best be handled by national action. The "States' Rights" supporters oppose such national action; they claim that these problems are of local concern and should be handled by the individual state governments. They believe that federal interference is unwarranted and unconstitutional. This major political problem has not yet been fully resolved.

Were senators originally elected directly by the people?

No, since senators were supposed to represent the states, they were elected originally by the state legislatures. The 17th Amendment, adopted in 1913, provides for the direct election of senators by the people of their states.

What amendment to the Constitution was subsequently repealed?

The 18th Amendment, which prohibited the manufacture or sale of intoxicating liquors, went into effect on January 16, 1920. It was repealed by the 21st Amendment on December 5, 1933.

What is the "lame duck" amendment?

The "lame duck" amendment is the 20th Amendment. It provides that the terms of the president and vice-president shall end at noon on January 20th, and the terms of senators and representatives shall end at noon on January 3rd. Prior to the adoption of the amendment in 1933, a congressman who failed to be reelected could serve from the first Monday in December until March 4th, and was called a "lame duck."

What is the presidential tenure amendment?

The presidential tenure amendment is the 22nd Amendment, which limits any one president's stay in office to two terms.

How many amendments are there to the Constitution?

There are 26 amendments to the Constitution of the United States.

What is the most recent amendment to the Constitution?

The 26th Amendment, ratified in 1971, is the most recent amendment. It lowered the minimum age for voting to 18 years.

Why is the Constitution considered to be a living document?

The Constitution of the United States is considered to be a living document because it has remained the basic law of the land for more than 200 years. While the Constitution itself remains the same, such changes as are necessary are made through amendments.

Is a proposed constitutional amendment submitted to the president for his approval?

No. A resolution proposing an amendment to the Constitution must be passed by a two-thirds vote of each house. It is not submitted to the president for his approval.

How can the Constitution be amended?

Amendments must be proposed by either a two-thirds vote of both houses of Congress or a national convention called by Congress upon the request of two-thirds of the state legislatures. Such proposal must then be ratified by either the legislatures of three-fourths of the states or special state conventions in three-fourths of the states.

Why is the Constitution called the supreme law of the land?

The Constitution is called the supreme law of the land because it is above any state law or any law passed by Congress. It is the highest law of the nation.

Documents of American Freedom

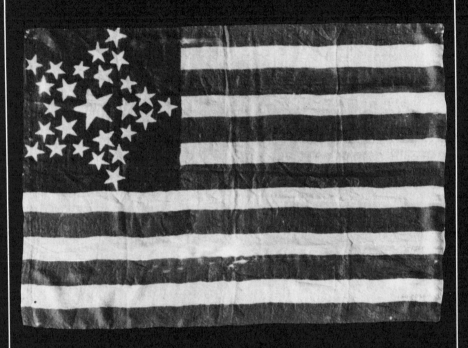

The Great Star Flag of twenty-six stars, With the increase in the number of
stars, the clearness of the stellar design was becoming lost, and it was felt that
a solution out of the difficulty was to group all the stars in one "great star".
The flag of twenty-six stars remained valid from 1837 to 1845.

The Mayflower Compact

This agreement, drawn up by the Pilgrims aboard the Mayflower on November 11, 1620, established the principle of democratic self-government in America.

In the name of God, Amen. We, whose names are underwritten, the loyal subjects of our dread sovereign Lord, King James, by the grace of God, of Great Britain, France, & Ireland, King, defender of the faith, etc., having undertaken for the glory of God and advancement of the Christian faith, and the honor of our King and country, a voyage to plant the first colony in the northern parts of Virginia, do by these presents, solemnly and mutually in the presence of God and one another, covenant and combine ourselves together into a civil body politic for our better ordering and preservation and furtherance of the ends aforesaid; and by virtue hereof do enact, constitute, and frame such just and equal laws, ordinances, acts, constitutions, and offices, from time to time, as shall be thought most meet and convenient for the general good of the colony; unto which we promise all due submission and obedience. In witness whereof we have hereunto subscribed our names at Cape Cod the eleventh of November, in the Reign of our Sovereign Lord King James of England, France, and Ireland, the eighteenth and of Scotland, the fifty-fourth. Anno Domini, 1620.

The Declaration of Independence
In Congress, July 4, 1776

The Unanimous Declaration of the Thirteen United States of America
(Simplified)

When in the course of human events, it becomes necessary for one people to dissolve the political bonds which have connected them with another, and to assume, among the powers of the earth, the separate and equal station to which the laws of nature and nature's God entitle them, a decent respect to the opinions of mankind requires that they should declare the causes which force them to the separation.

We hold these truths to be self-evident: That all men are created equal; that they are endowed by their Creator with certain unalienable rights; that among these are life, liberty, and the pursuit of happiness. That, to secure these rights, governments are instituted among men, deriving their just powers from the consent of the governed; that, whenever any form of government becomes destructive of these ends, it is the right of the people to alter or to abolish it, and to institute a new government, laying its foundation on such principles and organizing its powers in such form, as to them shall seem most likely to effect their safety and happiness. Prudence, indeed, will dictate that governments long established should not be changed for light or temporary causes; and accordingly, all experience has shown that mankind are more disposed to suffer, while evils are sufferable, than to right themselves by abolishing the forms to which they are accustomed. But when a long train of abuses and illegal actions, pursuing invariably the same object, shows a design to reduce them under absolute despotism, it is their right, it is their duty, to throw off such government, and to provide new guards for their future security. Such has been the patient suffering of these colonies; and such is now the necessity which compels them to alter their former systems of government. The history of the present King of Great Britain is a history of repeated injuries and illegal actions, all having in direct object the establishment of an absolute tyranny over these states. To prove this, let facts be submitted to an impartial world.

He has refused to consent to laws necessary for the public good.

He has forbidden his governors to pass laws of immediate and pressing importance.

He has refused to pass other laws for the accommodation of large districts of people, unless those people would give up their right of representation in the legislature.

He has called together legislative bodies at distant and inconvenient places for the purpose of tiring them into compliance with his measures.

He has dissolved representative houses for opposing his invasions on the people's rights.

He has refused, for a long time after such dissolutions, to permit others to be elected.

He has tried to prevent the population of these states from increasing by obstructing the naturalization laws, refusing to allow others to come, and raising the conditions of new appropriations of lands.

He has obstructed the administration of justice by not consenting to laws establishing judiciary powers.

He has made judges dependent on his will alone by controlling their salary and term of office.

He has created many new offices and appointed many officials to harass our people.

He has kept standing armies among us, in times of peace, without the consent of our legislatures.

He has tried to make the military free of civilian control.

He has combined with others to subject us to a jurisdiction foreign to our constitution, approving their acts of pretended legislation:

For quartering large bodies of armed troops among us;

For protecting them from punishment for any murders which they should commit on the inhabitants of these states;

For cutting off our trade with all parts of the world;

For imposing taxes on us without our consent;

For depriving us, in many cases, of the benefits of trial by jury;

For transporting us beyond seas to be tried for pretended offenses;

For establishing an arbitrary government in a neighboring province and threatening to introduce the same absolute rule into these colonies;

For taking away our charters, abolishing our laws, and changing the forms of our governments;

For suspending our own legislatures and assuming the power to legislate for us.

He has given up government here by declaring us out of his protection and waging war against us.

He has plundered our seas, ravaged our coasts, burned our towns, and destroyed the lives of our people.

He is at this time transporting large armies of foreign soldiers to complete the works of death, desolation, and tyranny.

He has captured our fellow citizens on the high seas and has forced them to bear arms against us.

He has aroused domestic uprisings amongst us.

In every stage of these oppressions, we have petitioned for redress in humble terms, but our repeated petitions have been answered only by repeated injury. A prince whose character is marked by every act which may define a tyrant is unfit to be the ruler of a free people.

Nor have we been wanting in our attentions to our British brothers. We have warned them repeatedly of attempts by their legislature to extend an unjust jurisdiction over us. We have reminded them of the circumstances of our emigration and settlement here. We have appealed to their native justice and generous spirit; and we have implored them, by the ties of our common relationship, to disclaim these illegal actions which would inevitably interrupt our connections and correspondence. They have also been deaf to the voice of justice and family relationships. We must, therefore, recognize the necessity which denounces our separation, and hold them, as we hold the rest of mankind, enemies in war, friends in peace.

We, therefore, the representatives of the United States of America, in General Congress assembled, appealing to the Supreme Judge of the world for the rectitude of our intentions, do, in the name and by the authority of the good people of these colonies, solemnly publish and declare that these united colonies are, and of right ought to be, free and independent states; that they are released from all allegiance to the British crown, and that all political connection between them and the state of Great Britain is, and ought to be, totally dissolved; and that, as free and independent states, they have full power to wage war, conclude peace, make alliances, establish commerce, and do all other acts and things which independent states may of right do. And for the support of this declaration, with a firm reliance on the protection of Divine Providence, we mutually pledge to each other our lives, our fortunes, and our sacred honor.

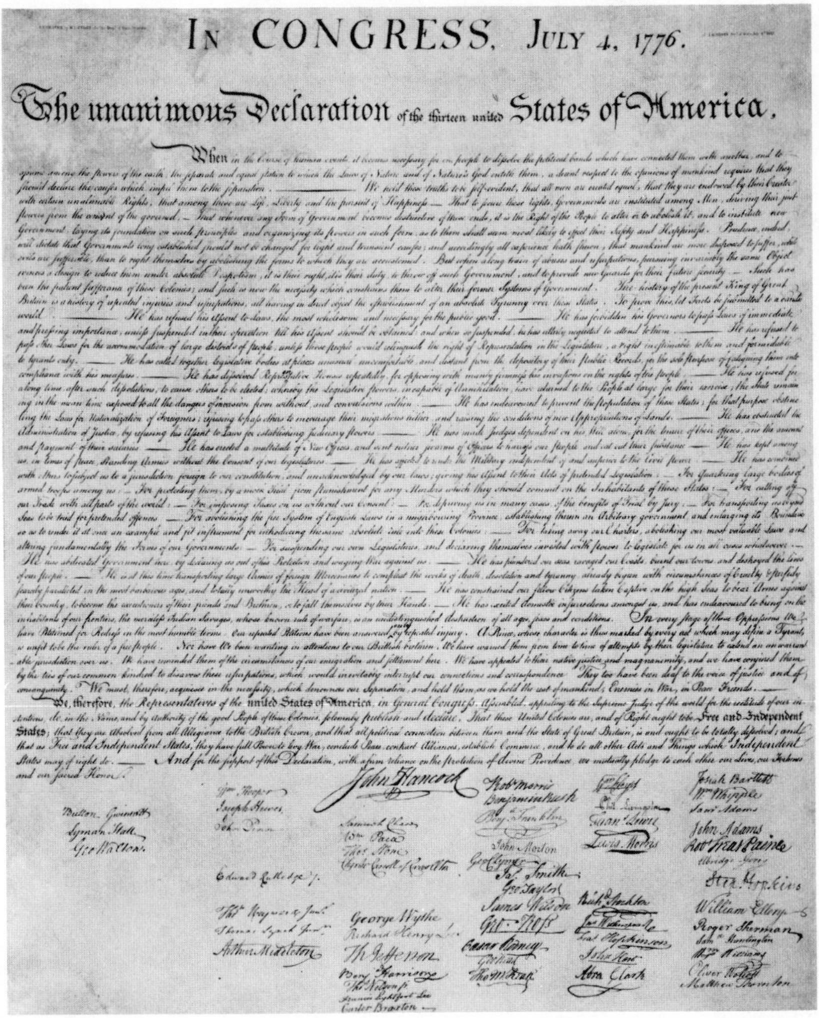

The Constitution
of the United States
# of America

Adopted September 17, 1787—Effective March 4, 1789 (Simplified)

Preamble

We, the people of the United States, in order to form a more perfect union, establish justice, insure domestic tranquility, provide for the common defense, promote the general welfare, and secure the blessings of liberty to ourselves and our posterity, do ordain and establish this Constitution for the United States of America.

Article I. The Legislative Department

Section 1. Congress

All legislative power shall be held by Congress which shall consist of a Senate and a House of Representatives.

Section 2. House of Representatives

1. The House of Representatives shall be composed of members elected by the people for two years.

2. A Representative must be 25 years old, a citizen of the United States for seven years and must live in the state where he is elected.

3. Representatives shall be apportioned among the states but shall not exceed one per 30,000 population. However, each state shall have at least one Representative. Indians who pay no taxes are excluded from the count, and five slaves shall be considered equal to three whites. Direct taxes shall also be apportioned among the states according to their population.* A census must be taken every ten years to determine the population.

4. When a vacancy occurs due to death, resignation, or any other cause, the Governor of the state shall call a special election to elect a new Representative.

5. The House of Representatives shall choose its Speaker and other officers. It shall have the power to impeach federal officials.

* Changed by the 16th Amendment.

Section 3. The Senate

1. The Senate shall be composed of two Senators from every state, chosen by the legislature for six years.*

2. One-third of the members shall be chosen every two years. If a vacancy occurs, the legislature shall elect a new Senator. If the legislature is not in session, the Governor shall make a temporary appointment until the next meeting of the legislature.

3. A Senator must be 30 years old, nine years a citizen of the United States and must live in the state where he is elected.

4. The Vice-President of the United States shall be the presiding officer of the Senate, but shall have a vote only in the event of a tie.

5. The Senate shall choose a president *pro tempore* who shall be the presiding officer in the absence of the Vice-President.

6. The Senate shall try officials impeached by the House of Representatives. A two-thirds vote is necessary for conviction. When the President of the United States is tried, the Chief Justice of the Supreme Court shall preside over the Senate.

7. When an official is convicted, the severest punishment that can be given is to remove him from office and disqualify him from holding any federal office. He may, however, be tried later and punished according to law.

Section 4. Election and Meetings of Congress

1. The legislature of each state shall prescribe the times, places, and manner of holding elections for Senators and Representatives. However, Congress may make or alter such regulations, except as to the places of choosing Senators.

2. Congress shall meet at least once a year beginning on the first Monday in December.* *

Section 5. Organization and Rules

1. Each House shall be the judge of the elections and qualifications of its own members. A majority of each House shall constitute a quorum to do business.

2. Each House may determine its rules, punish members for disorderly behavior and, by a two-thirds vote, expel a member.

* Changed by the 17th Amendment.
* * Changed by the 20th Amendment.

3. Each House shall publish a journal of its proceedings. No record need be kept of how each member votes on any question unless one-fifth of those present demand it.

4. Neither House shall adjourn for more than three days or meet in a different place without the consent of the other House.

Section 6. Privileges and Prohibitions

1. Senators and Representatives shall be paid for their services by the United States government. Unless charged with treason, felony or disorderly conduct, they cannot be arrested while going to, attending, or returning from a meeting of their House. They cannot be questioned about any statement made in Congress.

2. No Senator or Representative can hold another office in the government of the United States during his term of office.

Section 7. Method of Passing Laws

1. All bills for raising revenue must be introduced first in the House of Representatives, but the Senate may amend them.

2. After a bill has been passed by a majority vote of the House of Representatives and the Senate, it shall be submitted to the President of the United States. If he signs the bill, it becomes law. If he does not sign the bill, it shall be returned to the House where it originated for reconsideration. A two-thirds vote of both Houses is necessary to pass a law over the President's veto. If the President fails to act on a bill within ten days (Sundays excepted), it shall become law as if he had signed it. However, if Congress is not in session, and he does not act on the bill, it does not become a law.

3. Every resolution or vote which requires the agreement of the Senate and the House of Representatives (except the matter of adjournment) shall also require the approval of the President. If he disapproves, a two-thirds vote of the two Houses can override it.

Section 8. Powers of Congress

Congress shall have power:

1. To lay and collect taxes; to pay debts and to provide for the defense and welfare of the United States;

2. To borrow money;

3. To regulate commerce with foreign nations, among the states, and with the Indian tribes;

4. To establish naturalization laws and bankruptcy laws;

5. To coin money and fix the standard of weights and measures;

6. To provide punishment for counterfeiting United States bonds and money;

7. To establish post offices and post roads;

8. To promote science and art by granting patents and copyrights;

9. To establish courts lower than the Supreme Court;

10. To punish piracy, crimes committed on the high seas, and offenses against the law of nations;

11. To declare war;

12. To support an army;

13. To maintain a navy;

14. To regulate the land and naval forces;

15. To provide for calling forth the State Militia for employment in the service of the federal government;

16. To take care of the State Militia while it is employed in the service of the federal government;

17. To govern the Capital of the United States and all places bought from states for the purpose of erecting forts, dockyards, etc.; and

18. To make all laws which shall be necessary and proper for carrying out the foregoing powers, and all other powers vested by this Constitution in the government of the United States, or in any of its departments or officers.*

Section 9. Powers Denied to the United States

1. Congress may not prohibit the importation of slaves before 1808, but Congress may impose a tax on their importation of not more than $10 per person.

2. The writ of habeas corpus shall not be suspended except in cases of revolution or invasion.

3. No bill of attainder or ex post facto law shall be passed.

4. Direct taxes shall be levied among the states only in proportion to their population.* *

5. No tax shall be levied on exports.

6. No regulation of commerce or revenue may be passed giving preference to the ports of one state over those of another. No vessel shall be obliged to pay a tax if on its way from or to another state.

7. No money shall be drawn from the Treasury except according to an appropriation made by law. The Treasury shall publish a statement of its receipts and expenditures.

* Known as the Elastic Clause.
* * Changed by the 16th Amendment.

8. No title of nobility shall be granted by the United States. No person holding a federal office shall accept any present, compensation, office or title from any foreign country without the consent of Congress.

Section 10. Powers Denied to the States

1. No state shall make treaties, issue permission to capture foreign ships, coin or issue money, make anything but gold and silver legal tender in payment of debts, pass any bill of attainder or ex post facto law, or a law permitting a person to break a contract, or grant a title of nobility.

2. Without the consent of Congress, no state shall levy taxes on imports or exports, except what may be necessary for carrying out its inspection laws.

3. Without the consent of Congress, no state shall levy any tax on tonnage, keep troops or warships in time of peace, enter into any agreement with another state or with a foreign country, or engage in war, unless actually invaded or in immediate danger.

Article II. The Executive Department

Section 1. President and Vice-President

1. The chief executive shall be the President of the United States of America. He and the Vice-President shall hold office for four years and shall be elected in the following manner:

2. Each state shall appoint, in such manner as its legislature directs, a number of electors equal to the combined number of Senators and Representatives which the state sends to Congress. No Senator, Representative or any other person holding a federal office can be appointed an elector.

3. The electors shall meet in their states and vote for two persons for President. Their votes shall be sent to the presiding officer of the United States Senate who shall open them in the presence of the Senate and the House of Representatives and count them. The person having the largest number of votes, if that number is a majority of the total number of electors appointed, shall be elected President. The person having the second highest number of votes shall be elected Vice-President. If no one has a majority or if there is a tie, the House of Representatives shall elect a President, but in that case, each state has only one vote. If no Vice-President is elected by the electors, the United States Senate shall elect one.*

4. Congress may determine the time of choosing the electors and the day on which they shall hand in their votes, which day shall be the same throughout the United States.

* Changed completely by the 12th Amendment.

5. The President must be a natural born citizen of the United States. He must be 35 years old and must have been a resident of the United States for 14 years.

6. If the President's office is vacated through death, resignation or removal, or if the President is unable to perform his duties, the Vice-President shall take his place. If neither of them can act on account of death, resignation, removal or inability, Congress may provide which officer shall act as President.

7. The President shall be paid for his services. His salary cannot be increased or decreased during his term of office. He shall receive no other compensation from the federal or any state government.

8. On entering office, the President shall take the following oath:

"I do solemnly swear (or affirm) that I will faithfully execute the office of President of the United States, and will, to the best of my ability, preserve, protect, and defend the Constitution of the United States."

Section 2. Powers of the President

1. The President shall be the Commander-in-Chief of the Army and Navy of the United States, and of the State Militia when it is called into actual service of the United States. He may require the written opinion of the head of any executive department on matters relating to the duties of his office. He may pardon offenders against federal laws, except in cases of impeachment.

2. With the consent of two-thirds of the Senate, he may make treaties with foreign countries, appoint ambassadors and consuls, judges of the Supreme Court and other officers to fill places established by law.

3. When the Senate is not in session, the President may fill vacancies by appointment, which shall expire at the end of its next session.

Section 3. Duties of the President

He shall give to Congress information on the state of the union and recommend necessary legislation. He may call a special session of one or both Houses of Congress. He may decide when Congress should adjourn if the two Houses cannot agree on the date. He shall receive ambassadors and public ministers from foreign countries. He shall take care that the laws are faithfully executed, and shall commission all the officers of the United States.

Section 4. Impeachment

The President, Vice-President and all other officials of the United States shall be removed from office if they are impeached and convicted of treason, bribery or other serious crimes.

Article III. The Judicial Department

Section 1. The United States Courts

The United States judiciary shall consist of a Supreme Court and lower courts established by Congress. The Judges of the Supreme Court and of the lower courts shall hold office during good behavior, and shall be paid for their services. Their compensation cannot be diminished while they are in office.

Section 2. Jurisdiction

1. They shall try all cases involving violation of the Constitution, the laws of the United States or treaties made with foreign countries; all cases affecting ambassadors and other representatives from foreign countries; all admiralty and maritime cases; all cases involving the United States; all cases between two or more states, between a state and citizens of another state,* between citizens of different states, and between a state or its citizens and foreign states and their subjects.

2. In all cases involving ambassadors or other foreign representatives or those affecting a state, the Supreme Court shall have original jurisdiction. All other cases can come to the Supreme Court only on appeal from the lower courts.

3. All criminal trials, except cases of impeachment, shall be by jury and shall be held in the state where the crime was committed.

Section 3. Treason

1. Treason against the United States means carrying on war against it or helping its enemies. No person shall be convicted of treason unless on the testimony of two witnesses or on confession in open court.

2. Congress shall have power to declare the punishment for treason.

Article IV. Relations of the States

Section 1. Public Acts and Records

Each state shall consider as legal and proper the public acts, records and judicial decisions of every other state.

Section 2. Privileges of Citizens

1. The citizens of each state shall be entitled to all privileges of citizenship in all other states.

2. If a person charged with treason, felony or other crime in any state shall flee from justice to another state, he shall be delivered to the state where he is charged, on the demand of the governor of that state.

* Changed by the 11th Amendment.

3. A slave who escapes to another state does not become free but must be returned to his master.*

Section 3. New States and Territories

1. Congress may admit new states into this Union. No new state may be formed out of a part of another state or by joining parts of two or more states without the consent of the legislatures of the states concerned as well as of Congress.

2. Congress may govern and dispose of territory belonging to the United States.

Section 4. Protection to the States

The United States shall guarantee to every state in this Union a republican form of government, shall protect each of them against invasion, and ⋆ on application of the legislature or the Governor shall send troops to suppress domestic violence.

Article V. Amendments to the Constitution

When amendments are adopted, they shall be valid as any part of the Constitution. Amendments must be first proposed and then ratified by the states. They may be proposed in one of two ways: by a two-thirds vote in both Houses of Congress or by a convention called by Congress at the request of the legislatures of two-thirds of the states. They may be ratified in one of two ways: by the legislatures of three-fourths of the states or by conventions in three-fourths of the states. No amendment may be passed depriving a state, without its consent, of its two Senators.

Article VI. The Supreme Law of the Land

1. The United States shall pay all debts incurred before this Constitution was adopted.

2. This Constitution, the laws of the United States and all treaties made with foreign countries shall be the supreme law of the land, and no judge in any state can render a decision contrary to them.

3. Senators, Representatives, members of state legislatures and executive and judicial officers, both of the United States and of the individual states, shall take an oath to support this Constitution. No religious test shall be required as a qualification to any office in the United States.

Article VII. Ratification of the Constitution

The ratification of the conventions of nine states shall be sufficient for the establishment of this Constitution between the states so ratifying the same.

* Superseded by the 13th Amendment which prohibits slavery.

Amendments
to the
Constitution

(Amendments I-X, the Bill of Rights,—adopted 1791)

Amendment I. Religious and Political Freedom

Congress shall make no law establishing an official church or prohibiting free exercise of any religion, or limiting freedom of speech, of the press, or of the right of the people to assemble peaceably and to petition the government for redress of grievances.

Amendment II. Right to Keep and Bear Arms

Each state may maintain a militia for security purposes.

Amendment III. Quartering of Soldiers

In time of peace, no soldier shall be quartered in any house, without the consent of the owner.

Amendment IV. Search Warrants

People shall not be searched or seized unreasonably. Search warrants shall be issued only upon probable cause, supported by oath, and shall describe the place to be searched and the persons or things to be seized.

Amendment V. Right to Due Process of Law

No person shall be tried for a crime, unless he has been indicted by a grand jury; except at court-martial in time of war or public danger. No person can be tried for a crime the second time if he has been acquitted previously. No person shall be compelled to be a witness against himself in a criminal case. No person shall be deprived of life, liberty or property without due process of law. Private property shall not be taken for public use without just compensation.

Amendment VI. Rights of Accused Persons

In all criminal prosecutions, the accused shall have a speedy and public trial by an impartial jury in the state and district where the crime was committed. He must be informed of the nature and cause of the accusation. He must be confronted with the witnesses against him. He may compel witnesses to testify in his favor and may have a lawyer to assist in his defense.

Amendment VII. Trial by Jury in Civil Cases

In civil suits involving more than $20.00, persons are entitled to trial by jury.

Amendment VIII. Bails, Fines and Punishment

Excessive bail shall not be required, nor shall excessive fines be imposed, nor shall cruel and unusual punishment be inflicted.

Amendment IX. Rights Retained by the People

The stating in the Constitution of certain rights guaranteed to the people shall not be taken to mean that they have no other rights.

Amendment X. Rights Reserved to the States

The powers not given to the United States by the Constitution, nor prohibited by it to the states, are reserved to the states or to the people.

Amendment XI. Limiting Powers of Federal Courts (Adopted 1798)

The federal courts shall have no jurisdiction in cases in which a state is sued by a citizen of another state or by a citizen of a foreign country.

Amendment XII. Election of President and Vice-President (Adopted 1804)

1. The electors shall meet in their states and vote separately for President and Vice-President. The results of their votes shall be sent to the presiding officer of the United States Senate who shall open them in the presence of the Senate and the House of Representatives and count them. The person having the largest number of votes for President, if that number is a majority of the total number of electors appointed, shall be President. The person having the largest number of votes for Vice-President, if that number is a majority of the total number of electors appointed, shall be Vice-President.

2. If no person has such majority for President of the United States, the top three persons only will be considered. The House of Representatives shall elect a President by majority vote, each state having only one vote. If no person has such majority for Vice-President, the top two persons will be considered. The Senate shall elect a Vice-President.

3. The Vice-President must have the same qualifications as are required for the office of the President.

Amendment XIII. Slavery Abolished (Adopted 1865)

No slavery or involuntary servitude, except as punishment for a crime, shall exist within the United States or in any place subject to its laws.

Amendment XIV. Citizenship Granted to Negroes (Adopted 1868)

1. All persons born or naturalized in the United States and subject to its laws are citizens of the United States and of the state in which they live. No state shall make any law which shall abridge the privileges of the citizens of the United States; nor shall any state deprive any person of life, liberty or property without due process of law; nor deny any person equal protection of the law.

2. If any state deprives any male citizens over 21 years of age of the right to vote, these citizens shall not be counted in deciding the number of Representatives that state should send to Congress.

3. No person who as a federal or state official took an oath to support the Constitution of the United States, and later took part in any rebellion against the United States, can hold any federal or state office, civil or military. However, Congress may remove such disability by a two-thirds vote of each House.

4. Neither the United States nor any state shall pay any debt incurred in aiding a rebellion against the United States or any claim for the loss or emancipation of slaves. All such debts are illegal and void.

Amendment XV. Negro Suffrage (Adopted 1870)

The right of citizens of the United States to vote shall not be denied to anyone by the United States or by any state on account of race, color or previous condition of servitude.

Amendment XVI. Income Tax (Adopted 1913)

Congress shall have power to levy and collect income taxes without apportioning them among the states according to their population.

Amendment XVII. Popular Election of Senators (Adopted 1913)

1. United States Senators shall be elected by the people of each state.

2. When a vacancy occurs in the Senate, the Governor of the state shall call a special election to fill the vacancy. The legislature of the state may empower the Governor to make a temporary appointment until a new Senator is elected.

Amendment XVIII. National Prohibition (Adopted 1920)

The manufacture, sale, transportation, exportation and importation of intoxicating liquors for drinking purposes is forbidden in the United States and in all territory under its laws.*

Amendment XIX. Woman Suffrage (Adopted 1920)

The right of citizens of the United States to vote shall not be denied by the United States or any state on account of sex.

Amendment XX. Change of Congressional and Presidential Terms (Adopted 1933)

1. The terms of the President and Vice-President shall end at noon on the 20th day of January, and the terms of Senators and Representatives at noon on the 3rd day of January, of the years in which such terms would have ended if this amendment had not been ratified; and the terms of their successors shall then begin.

* Superseded by the 21st Amendment.

2. Congress shall assemble at least once every year, and such meeting shall begin at noon on the 3rd day of January, unless they shall by law appoint a different day.

3. If, at the time fixed for the beginning of the term of the President, the President-elect shall have died, the Vice President-elect shall become President.

Amendment XXI. Repeal of Prohibition (Adopted 1933)

1. The 18th amendment to the Constitution of the United States is hereby repealed.

2. The transportation or importation into any state, territory or possession of the United States for delivery or use therein of intoxicating liquors, in violation of the laws thereof, is hereby prohibited.

Amendment XXII. Two-Term Limitation (Adopted 1951)

No person shall be elected to the office of the President more than twice, and no person who has held the office of President, or acted as President, for more than two years of a term to which some other person was elected President shall be elected to the office of the President more than once.

Amendment XXIII. Presidential Electors for District of Columbia (Adopted 1961)

The District of Columbia shall appoint a number of electors of President and Vice-President equal to the total number of Senators and Representatives in Congress to which the District would be entitled if it were a state. However, the District's electoral vote, regardless of its population, shall be limited to the number of electoral votes of the least populous state. These electors shall meet in the District and perform such duties as provided by the 12th amendment.

Amendment XXIV. Poll Tax Barred in Federal Elections (Adopted 1964)

The right of citizens of the United States to vote in any primary or other election for President or Vice-President, for electors for President or Vice-President, or for Senator or Representative in Congress, shall not be denied or abridged by the United States or any State by reason of failure to pay any poll tax or other tax.

Amendment XXV. Presidential Disability and Succession (Adopted 1967)

1. In case of the removal of the President from office or his death or resignation, the Vice-President shall become President.

2. Whenever there is a vacancy in the office of the Vice-President, the President shall nominate a Vice-President who shall take office upon confirmation by a majority of both Houses of Congress.

3. Whenever the President transmits to the President *pro tempore* of the Senate and the Speaker of the House of Representatives his written declaration that he is unable to discharge the powers and duties of his office, and until he transmits to them a written declaration to the contrary, such powers and duties shall be discharged by the Vice-President as Acting President.

4. Whenever the Vice-President and a majority of either the principal officers of the executive departments or of such other body as Congress may by law provide, transmit to the President *pro tempore* of the Senate and the Speaker of the House of Representatives their written declaration that the President is unable to discharge the powers and duties of his office, the Vice-President shall immediately assume the powers and duties of the office as Acting President.

Thereafter, when the President transmits to the President *pro tempore* of the Senate and the Speaker of the House of Representatives his written declaration that no inability exists, he shall resume the powers and duties of his office unless the Vice-President and a majority of either the principal officers of the executive department or of such other body as Congress may by law provide, transmit within four days to the President *pro tempore* of the Senate and the Speaker of the House of Representatives their written declaration that the President is unable to discharge the powers and duties of his office. Thereupon Congress shall decide the issue, assembling within 48 hours for that purpose if not in session. If the Congress, within 21 days after receipt of the latter written declaration, or, if Congress is not in session, within 21 days after Congress is required to assemble, determines by two-thirds vote of both houses that the President is unable to discharge the powers and duties of his office, the Vice-President shall continue to discharge the same as Acting President; otherwise, the President shall resume the powers and duties of his office.

Amendment XXVI. Lowering Voting Age to 18 Years (Adopted 1971)

1. The right of citizens of the United States, who are 18 years of age or older, to vote shall not be denied or abridged by the United States or any state on account of age.

2. The Congress shall have the power to enforce this article by appropriate legislation.

The Gettysburg Address

Delivered by President Abraham Lincoln at the Dedication of the National Cemetery at the site of the battle of Gettysburg, November 19, 1863.

Fourscore and seven years ago, our fathers brought forth on this continent a new nation, conceived in liberty, and dedicated to the proposition that all men are created equal.

Now we are engaged in a great civil war, testing whether that nation, or any nation so conceived and so dedicated, can long endure. We are met on a great battlefield of that war. We have come to dedicate a portion of that field as a final resting place for those who here gave their lives that that nation might live. It is altogether fitting and proper that we should do this.

But, in a larger sense, we cannot dedicate, we cannot consecrate, we cannot hallow this ground. The brave men, living and dead, who struggled here, have consecrated it far above our poor power to add or detract. The world will little note nor long remember what we say here, but it can never forget what they did here. It is for us the living, rather, to be dedicated here to the unfinished work which they who fought here have thus far so nobly advanced. It is rather for us to be here dedicated to the great task remaining before us—that from these honored dead we take increased devotion to that cause for which they gave the last full measure of devotion; that we here highly resolve that these dead shall not have died in vain; that this nation, under God, shall have a new birth of freedom; and that government of the people, by the people, for the people, shall not perish from the earth.

The Four Freedoms

The "Four Freedoms" were stated in the President's annual message to Congress which was delivered by President Franklin D. Roosevelt on January 6, 1941. They were accepted as the most concise statement of the ideals for which Americans were prepared to fight.

In the future days, which we seek to make secure, we look forward to a world founded upon four essential human freedoms.

The first is the freedom of speech and expression—everywhere in the world.

The second is freedom of every person to worship God in his own way —everywhere in the world.

The third is freedom from want—which, translated into world terms, means economic understandings which will secure to every nation a healthy peacetime life for its inhabitants—everywhere in the world.

The fourth is freedom from fear—which, translated into world terms, means a world-wide reduction of armaments to such a point and in such a thorough fashion that no nation will be in a position to commit an act of physical aggression against any neighbor—anywhere in the world.

That is no vision of a distant millennium. It is a definite basis for the kind of world attainable in our own time and generation.

Preamble to the
Charter of the United Nations

The preamble to the Charter of the United Nations lays down the fundamental principles and expresses the ideals under which the United Nations
was established as a world-wide organization. The Charter was adopted in
San Francisco on June 26, 1945.

We, the people of the United Nations, determined to save succeeding
generations from the scourge of war, which twice in our lifetime has
brought untold sorrow to mankind, and

To reaffirm faith in fundamental human rights, in the dignity and worth
of the human person, in the equal rights of men and women and of the
nations large and small, and

To establish conditions under which justice and respect for the obligations arising from treaties and other sources of international law can be
maintained, and

To promote social progress and better standards of life in larger freedom,
and for these ends

To promote tolerance and live together in peace with one another as
good neighbors, and

To unite our strength to maintain international peace and security, and

To ensure, by the acceptance of principles and the institution of meth-
ods, that armed force shall not be used, save in the common interest, and

To employ international machinery for the promotion of the economic
and social advancement of all peoples, have resolved to combine our efforts
to accomplish these aims.

Accordingly, our respective governments, through representatives assembled in the City of San Francisco, who have exhibited their full powers
found to be in good and due form, have agreed to the present Charter of
the United Nations and do hereby establish an international organization
to be known as the United Nations.

American Patriotic Literature

The Kingsboro Eagle Flag of twenty-six stars was painted by an artist named "Holmes", who proudly signed his creation on the eagle's tail feathers. "Eagle flags" were used by consulates and other governmental agencies and offices. Circa 1840.

The Oath of Allegiance
(taken when naturalized)

"I hereby declare, on oath, that I absolutely and entirely renounce and abjure all allegiance and fidelity to any foreign prince, potentate, state, or sovereignty of whom or which I have heretofore been a subject or citizen; that I will support and defend the Constitution and laws of the United States of America against all enemies, foreign and domestic; that I will bear true faith and allegiance to the same; that I will bear arms on behalf of the United States or perform noncombatant service in the Armed Forces of the United States when required by law; and that I take this obligation freely without any mental reservation or purpose of evasion; so help me God."

If the petitioner is opposed to bearing of arms or the performance of non-combatant service in the Armed Forces of the United States by reason of religious training, he is allowed to delete that portion from the oath.

The Pledge of Allegiance

"I pledge allegiance to the flag of the United States of America and to the Republic for which it stands, one nation under God, indivisible, with liberty and justice for all."

The Star-Spangled Banner
(The National Anthem)

Oh say, can you see, by the dawn's early light,
What so proudly we hailed at the twilight's last gleaming?
Whose broad stripes and bright stars, through the perilous fight,
O'er the ramparts we watched, were so gallantly streaming!
And the rockets' red glare, the bombs bursting in air,
Gave proof through the night that our flag was still there.
Oh say, does that star-spangled banner yet wave
O'er the land of the free and the home of the brave?

On the shore, dimly seen through the mists of the deep,
Where the foe's haughty host in dread silence reposes,
What is that which the breeze, o'er the towering steep,
As it fitfully blows, half conceals, half discloses?
Now it catches the gleam of the morning's first beam,
In full glory reflected now shines on the stream.
'Tis the star-spangled banner! Oh long may it wave
O'er the land of the free and the home of the brave.

Oh! thus be it ever, when freemen shall stand
Between their loved homes and the war's desolation.
Blest with victory and peace, may the Heaven-rescued land
Praise the Power that hath made and preserved us a nation.
Then conquer we must, for our cause it is just,
And this be our motto: "In God is our trust."
And the star-spangled banner in triumph shall wave
O'er the land of the free and the home of the brave.

FRANCIS SCOTT KEY

America

My country, 'tis of thee
Sweet land of liberty,
Of thee I sing;
Land where my fathers died,
Land of the Pilgrims' pride,
From every mountain-side
Let Freedom ring.

My native country, thee—
Land of the noble free,—
Thy name I love;
I love thy rocks and rills,
Thy woods and templed hills;
My heart with rapture thrills
Like that above.

Let music swell the breeze,
And ring from all the trees
Sweet freedom's song;
Let mortal tongues awake,
Let all that breathe partake,
Let rocks their silence break,—
The sound prolong. .

Our fathers' God, to Thee,
Author of liberty,
To Thee we sing;
Long may our land be bright,
With Freedom's holy light;
Protect us by Thy might,
Great God, our King!

SAMUEL FRANCIS SMITH

America the Beautiful

O beautiful for spacious skies,
    For amber waves of grain,—
For purple mountain majesties
    Above the fruited plain.

America! America!
    God shed His grace on thee,—
And crown thy good with brotherhood,
    From sea to shining sea.

O beautiful for pilgrim feet,
    Whose stern impassioned stress—
A thoroughfare for freedom beat
    Across the wilderness.

America! America!
    God mend thine ev'ry flaw,—
Confirm thy soul in self-control,
    Thy liberty in law.

O beautiful for heroes proved
    In liberating strife,—
Who more than self their country loved,
    And mercy more than life.

America! America!
    May God thy gold refine—
Till all success by nobleness,
    And every gain divine.

O beautiful for patriot dream
    That sees beyond the years—
Thine alabaster cities gleam
    Undimmed by human tears.

America! America!
    God shed His grace on thee,—
And crown thy good with brotherhood,
    From sea to shining sea.

KATHARINE LEE BATES

God Bless America*

While the storm clouds gather
Far across the sea,
Let us swear allegiance
To a land that's free;
Let us all be grateful
For a land so fair,
As we raise our voices
In a solemn prayer.

God bless America,
Land that I love,
Stand beside her and guide her
Thru the night with a light from above;
From the mountains, to the prairies,
To the oceans white with foam,
God bless America
My home sweet home.

IRVING BERLIN

Concord Hymn

This poem was written in praise of the members of the militia who fought the first battle of the American Revolutionary War at Concord, Massachusetts, in 1775.

Although the bridge is no longer standing, a statue has been erected in its place to serve as a battle monument. Concord Hymn was sung at the unveiling of the statue in 1836.

By the rude bridge that arched the flood,
Their flag to April's breeze unfurled,
Here once the embattled farmers stood
And fired the shot heard round the world.

The foe long since in silence slept;
Alike the conqueror silent sleeps:
And Time the ruined bridge has swept
Down the dark stream which seaward creeps.

On this green bank, by this soft stream,
We set today a votive stone;
That memory may their deed redeem,
When, like our sires, our sons are gone.

Spirit, that made those heroes dare
To die, and leave their children free,
Bid Time and Nature gently spare
The shaft we raise to them and thee.

RALPH WALDO EMERSON

The Flag Goes By

This poem describes the thoughts and feelings of Americans as the flag passes by. They view the flag as a symbol of America's heroic past and hope for a glorious future—a land which has enabled them to realize their dreams and aspirations. It is a feeling of awe and respect for their country, as well as pride in her accomplishments, that makes them take their hats off when the flag goes by.

> *Hats off!*
> *Along the street there comes*
> *A blare of bugles, a ruffle of drums,*
> *A flash of color beneath the sky:*
> *Hats off!*
> *The flag is passing by!*

Blue and crimson and white it shines,
Over the steel-tipped, ordered lines.
    Hats off!
The colors before us fly;
But more than the flag is passing by.

Sea-fights and land-fights, grim and great,
Fought to make and to save the State;
Weary marches and sinking ships;
Cheers of victory on dying lips;

Days of plenty and years of peace;
March of a strong land's swift increase;
Equal justice, right and law,
Stately honor and reverend awe;

Sign of a nation, great and strong
To ward her people from foreign wrong:
Pride and glory and honor,—all
Live in the colors to stand or fall.

    Hats off!
Along the streets there comes
A blare of bugles, a ruffle of drums;
And loyal hearts are beating high:
    Hats off!
The flag is passing by!

HENRY HOLCOMB BENNETT

The Ship of State

The poet compares our nation to a ship starting on a long voyage. He cautions the ship not to fear the dangers of the sea because our "ship of state" is not only strong and well-built, but it has the support, faith and hope of its people.

Thou, too, sail on, O Ship of State!
Sail on, O Union, strong and great!
Humanity with all its fears,
With all the hopes of future years,
Is hanging breathless on thy fate!

We know what Master laid thy keel,
What Workmen wrought thy ribs of steel,
Who made each mast, and sail, and rope,
What anvils rang, what hammers beat,
In what a force and what a heat
Were shaped the anchors of thy hope!

Fear not each sudden sound and shock,
'Tis of the wave and not the rock;
'Tis but the flapping of the sail,
And not a rent made by the gale!

In spite of rock and tempest's roar,
In spite of false lights on the shore,
Sail on, nor fear to breast the sea!

Our hearts, our hopes, are all with thee,
Our hearts, our hopes, our prayers, our tears,
Our faith triumphant o'er our fears,
Are all with thee—are all with thee!

HENRY W. LONGFELLOW

Old Ironsides

The Constitution, better known as Old Ironsides, was a famous American warship. She was in many battles during the War of 1812. In 1830, she was condemned as being no longer fit for combat. Publication of this poem aroused the public's indignation and The Constitution was rebuilt instead of being discarded.

Ay, tear her tattered ensign down!
   Long has it waved on high,
And many an eye has danced to see
   The banner in the sky;
Beneath it rung the battle shout,
   And burst the cannon's roar;—

The meteor of the ocean air
   Shall sweep the clouds no more.
Her decks, once red with heroes' blood,
   Where knelt the vanquished foe,
When winds were hurrying o'er the flood,
   And waves were white below,
No more shall feel the victor's tread,
   Or know the conquered knee:
The harpies of the shore shall pluck
   The eagle of the sea!

Oh, better that her shattered hulk
   Should sink beneath the wave;
Her thunders shook the mighty deep,
   And there should be her grave;
Nail to the mast her holy flag,
   Set every threadbare sail,
And give her to the god of storms,
   The lightning and the gale!

OLIVER WENDELL HOLMES

O Captain! My Captain!

In this poem, Abraham Lincoln is pictured as a captain of a ship that he has just brought safely through the storm of the Civil War. The people, waiting on shore for the safe return of the storm-tossed vessel, are eager to give their victorious leader a hearty welcome. Instead, they find him dead.

O Captain! my Captain! our fearful trip is done,
The ship has weather'd every rack, the prize we sought is won;
The port is near, the bells I hear, the people all exulting,
While follow eyes the steady keel, the vessel grim and daring:
    But O heart! heart! heart!
      O the bleeding drops of red,
        Where on the deck my Captain lies,
        Fallen and cold and dead!

O Captain! my Captain! rise up and hear the bells;
Rise up—for you the flag is flung—for you the bugle trills;
For you bouquets and ribbon'd wreaths—for you the shores a-
   crowding;
For you they call, the swaying mass, their eager faces turning;
    Here Captain! dear father!
      This arm beneath your head!
      It is some dream that on the deck
        You've fallen cold and dead.

My Captain does not answer, his lips are pale and still,
My father does not feel my arm, he has no pulse nor will:
The ship is anchor'd safe and sound, its voyage closed and done,
From fearful trip the victor ship comes in with object won:
    Exult, O shores and ring, O bells!
      But I, with mournful tread,
        Walk the deck my Captain lies,
        Fallen cold and dead.

WALT WHITMAN

I Hear America Singing

The poet describes a happy America engaging in different tasks. People with varied skills perform their work with enthusiasm, joy and satisfaction.

I hear America singing, the varied carols I hear,
Those of mechanics, each one singing his as it should be blithe and strong,
The carpenter singing his as he measures his plank or beam,
The mason singing his as he makes ready for work, or leaves off work,
The boatman singing what belongs to him in his boat, the deckhand
*   singing on the steamboat deck,*
The shoemaker singing as he sits on his bench, the hatter singing as he
*   stands,*
The wood-cutter's song, the ploughboy's on his way in the morning, or at
*   noon intermission or at sundown,*
The delicious singing of the mother, or of the young wife at work, or of the
*   girl sewing or washing,*
Each singing what belongs to him or her and to none else,
The day what belongs to the day—at night the party of young fellows,
*   robust, friendly,*
Singing with open mouths their strong, melodious songs.

WALT WHITMAN

America for Me

The poet admires the beauty and charm of the Old World with its rich heritage and glorious past. However, he prefers America with its promising future and is anxious to return to our country—the land of freedom and opportunity.

'Tis fine to see the Old World, and travel up and down
Among the famous palaces and cities of renown,
To admire the crumbly castles and the statues of the kings,—
But now I think I've had enough of antiquated things.

So it's home again, and home again, America for me!
My heart is turning home again, and there I long to be,
In the land of youth and freedom beyond the ocean bars,
Where the air is full of sunlight and the flag is full of stars.

Oh, London is a man's town, there's power in the air;
And Paris is a woman's town, with flowers in her hair;
And it's sweet to dream in Venice, and it's great to study Rome;
But when it comes to living, there is no place like Home.

I like the German fir-woods, in green battalions drilled;
I like the gardens of Versailles with flashing fountains filled;
But, oh, to take your hand, my dear, and ramble for a day
In the friendly western woodland where Nature has her way!

I know that Europe's wonderful, yet something seems to lack;
The Past is too much with her, and the people looking back,
But the glory of the Present is to make the Future free,—
We love our land for what she is and what she is to be.

Oh, it's home again, and home again, America for me!
I want a ship that's westward bound to plough the rolling sea
To the blessed land of Room Enough beyond the ocean bars,
Where the air is full of sunlight and the flag is full of stars.

HENRY VAN DYKE

Nearly 10,000 U.S. sailors posed in a Chicago parade ground as photographer Arthur S. Mole took this photo of the "living flag" in 1917.

I Am an American

The first part of this poem tells about the feelings of a boy whose ancestors helped build this country; the second part expresses the thoughts of a young immigrant whose ancestors suffered many hardships under despotic rule. Despite their different backgrounds, each is proud of his past, proud of the future, and proud to say, "I am an American."

I am an American.
My father belongs to the Sons of the Revolution;
My mother, to the Colonial Dames.
One of my ancestors pitched·tea overboard in Boston Harbor;
Another stood his ground with Warren;
Another hungered with Washington at Valley Forge.
My forefathers were America in the making:
They spoke in her council halls;
They died on her battle-fields;
They commanded her ships;
They cleared her forests.
Dawns reddened and paled.
Stanch hearts of mine beat fast at each new star in the nation's flag.

Keen eyes of mine foresaw her greater victory:
The sweep of her seas,
The plenty of her plains,
The man-hives in her billion-wired cities.
Every drop of blood in me holds a heritage of patriotism.
I am proud of my past.
I am an American.

I am an American.
My father was an atom of dust,
My mother a straw in the wind,
To His Serene Majesty.
One of my ancestors died in the mines of Siberia;
Another was crippled for life by twenty blows of the knout;
The history of my ancestors is a trail of blood to the palace-gate of the
    Great White Czar.
But then the dream came—
The dream of America.
In the light of the Liberty torch,
The atom of dust became a man,
And the straw in the wind became a woman for the first time.
"See," said my father, pointing to the flag that fluttered near,
"That flag of stars and stripes is yours;
It is the emblem of the promised land.
It means, my son, the hope of humanity.
Live for it—die for it!"
Under the open sky of my new country, I swore to do so;
And every drop of blood in me will keep that vow.
I am proud of my future.
I am an American.

ELIAS LIEBERMAN

The New Colossus

This poem is engraved on a tablet at the base of the Statue of Liberty.

Not like the brazen giant of Greek fame,
With conquering limbs astride from land to land;
Here at our sea-washed, sunset gates shall stand
A mighty woman with a torch, whose flame
Is the imprisoned lightning, and her name
Mother of Exiles. From her beacon-hand
Glows world-wide welcome; her mild eyes command
The air-bridged harbor that twin cities frame.
"Keep ancient lands, your storied pomp!" cries she
With silent lips. "Give me your tired, your poor,
Your huddled masses yearning to breathe free,
The wretched refuse of your teeming shore.
Send these, the homeless, tempest-tost to me,
I lift my lamp beside the golden door!"

EMMA LAZARUS

The American's Creed

The author selected phrases from various American documents and combined them into a creed—an expression of an American's belief and faith in the ideals and aspirations of our country.

I believe in the United States of America as a government of the people, by the people, for the people; whose just powers are derived from the consent of the governed; a democracy in a republic; a sovereign nation of many sovereign states; a perfect Union, one and inseparable; established upon those principles of freedom, equality, justice, and humanity for which American patriots sacrificed their lives and fortunes.

I therefore believe it is my duty to my country to love it; to support its constitution; to obey its laws; to respect its flag; and to defend it against all enemies.

WILLIAM TYLER PAGE

The Dodge Flag of thirty-three stars was made on the eve of the Civil War by a pioneer family traveling west in a covered wagon.

Presidents of the United States

Name	Term	Elected From	Occupation	Political Party
1. George Washington	1789-1797	Virginia	Planter	....
2. John Adams	1797-1801	Massachusetts	Lawyer	Federalist
3. Thomas Jefferson	1801-1809	Virginia	Planter	Dem.-Rep.
4. James Madison	1809-1817	Virginia	Public Official	Dem.-Rep.
5. James Monroe	1817-1825	Virginia	Lawyer	Dem.-Rep.
6. John Quincy Adams	1825-1829	Massachusetts	Lawyer	Nat. Rep.
7. Andrew Jackson	1829-1837	Tennessee	Lawyer	Democratic
8. Martin Van Buren	1837-1841	New York	Lawyer	Democratic
9. William H. Harrison	1841	Ohio	Farmer	Whig
10. John Tyler	1841-1845	Virginia	Lawyer	Whig
11. James Knox Polk	1845-1849	Tennessee	Lawyer	Democratic
12. Zachary Taylor	1849-1850	Louisiana	Soldier	Whig
13. Millard Fillmore	1850-1853	New York	Lawyer	Whig
14. Franklin Pierce	1853-1857	New Hampshire	Lawyer	Democratic
15. James Buchanan	1857-1861	Pennsylvania	Lawyer	Democratic
16. Abraham Lincoln	1861-1865	Illinois	Lawyer	Republican
17. Andrew Johnson	1865-1869	Tennessee	Tailor	Republican
18. Ulysses S. Grant	1869-1877	Illinois	Soldier	Republican
19. Rutherford B. Hayes	1877-1881	Ohio	Lawyer	Republican
20. James A. Garfield	1881	Ohio	Lawyer	Republican
21. Chester A. Arthur	1881-1885	New York	Lawyer	Republican
22. Grover Cleveland	1885-1889	New York	Lawyer	Democratic
23. Benjamin Harrison	1889-1893	Indiana	Lawyer	Republican
24. Grover Cleveland	1893-1897	New York	Lawyer	Democratic
25. William McKinley	1897-1901	Ohio	Lawyer	Republican
26. Theodore Roosevelt	1901-1909	New York	Public Official	Republican
27. William H. Taft	1909-1913	Ohio	Lawyer	Republican
28. Woodrow Wilson	1913-1921	New Jersey	Educator	Democratic
29. Warren G. Harding	1921-1923	Ohio	Editor	Republican
30. Calvin Coolidge	1923-1929	Massachusetts	Lawyer	Republican
31. Herbert Hoover	1929-1933	California	Engineer	Republican
32. Franklin D. Roosevelt	1933-1945	New York	Lawyer	Democratic
33. Harry S Truman	1945-1953	Missouri	Public Official	Democratic
34. Dwight D. Eisenhower	1953-1961	New York	Soldier	Republican
35. John F. Kennedy	1961-1963	Massachusetts	Public Official	Democratic
36. Lyndon B. Johnson	1963-1969	Texas	Public Official	Democratic
37. Richard M. Nixon	1969-1974	New York	Lawyer	Republican
38. Gerald R. Ford	1974-1977	Michigan	Public Official	Republican
39. Jimmy (James E.) Carter	1977-1981	Georgia	Businessman	Democratic
40. Ronald W. Reagan	1981-	California	Public Official	Republican

Other Famous Americans

Samuel Adams (1722-1803), patriot during the American Revolutionary War

Jane Addams (1860-1935), social worker—founded Hull House

Louis Agassiz (1807-1873), biologist and educator

Louisa May Alcott (1832-1888), writer of children's stories

Susan B. Anthony (1820-1906), crusader for women's rights

John James Audubon (1785-1851), naturalist and artist

Clara Barton (1821-1912), educator and social worker—helped establish the American Red Cross

Alexander Graham Bell (1847-1922), inventor of the telephone

Daniel Boone (1734-1820), explorer and pioneer—helped in the westward expansion

Louis D. Brandeis (1856-1941), jurist

William Jennings Bryan (1860-1925), orator and statesman

William Cullen Bryant (1794-1878), poet and editor

Pearl S. Buck (1892-1973), novelist

Luther Burbank (1849-1926), agriculturist and plant scientist

Richard E. Byrd (1888-1957), explorer—flew over both the North and South Poles

John C. Calhoun (1782-1850), orator and statesman

Andrew Carnegie (1835-1919), industrialist and philanthropist

George Washington Carver (1864-1943), scientist and educator

Henry Clay (1777-1852), orator and statesman—known as the "Great Compromiser"

Samuel L. Clemens (Mark Twain) (1835-1910), author

Arthur H. Compton (1892-1962), physicist

James Fenimore Cooper (1789-1851), novelist

Peter Cooper (1791-1883), industrialist and philanthropist—founded Cooper Union

Jefferson Davis (1808-1889), president of the Confederate States during the Civil War

John Dewey (1859-1952), philosopher and educator

Mary Baker Eddy (1821-1910), religious leader—founder of Christian Science

Thomas A. Edison (1847-1931), inventor of the electric light, phonograph, motion picture machine, etc.

Albert Einstein (1879-1955), physicist and mathematician

Ralph Waldo Emerson (1803-1882), poet and philosopher

Enrico Fermi (1901-1954), physicist —helped develop the atom bomb

F. Scott Fitzgerald (1896-1949), novelist

Henry Ford (1863-1947), industrialist—introduced mass production of the automobile

Stephen Foster (1826-1864), composer

Benjamin Franklin (1706-1790), patriot, statesman, inventor and publisher—wrote *Poor Richard's Almanac*

Robert Fulton (1765-1815), inventor of the steamboat

George Gershwin (1898-1937), composer

Josiah W. Gibbs (1839-1903), physicist

George W. Goethals (1858-1928), army engineer—built the Panama Canal

Samuel Gompers (1850-1924), labor leader—first president of the American Federation of Labor

Charles Goodyear (1800-1860), inventor—vulcanized rubber

William C. Gorgas (1854-1920), army surgeon—fought against yellow fever and malaria

Nathan Hale (1755-1776), American patriot executed by the British during the American Revolutionary War

Alexander Hamilton (1757-1804), patriot and statesman—first Secretary of the Treasury

Nathaniel Hawthorne (1804-1864), author

Patrick Henry (1736-1799), orator and patriot

Victor Herbert (1859-1924), composer

Oliver Wendell Holmes (1841-1935), jurist

Mark Hopkins (1802-1887), educator

Elias Howe (1819-1867), inventor of the sewing machine

Washington Irving (1783-1859), historian, essayist and story writer

John Jay (1745-1829), jurist and statesman

John Paul Jones (1747-1792), naval commander during the American Revolutionary War

Jerome D. Kern (1885-1945), composer

Martin Luther King, Jr. (1929-1968), civil rights leader

Karl Landsteiner (1883-1943), scientist—discoverer of human blood groups

Robert E. Lee (1807-1870), Commander-in-Chief of the Confederate Army during the Civil War

John L. Lewis (1880-1969), labor leader—organized the Congress of Industrial Organizations

Henry W. Longfellow (1807-1882), poet

Douglas MacArthur (1880-1964), Supreme Commander in the Pacific during World War II

Horace Mann (1796-1859), educator—founded the American public school system

John Marshall (1755-1835), jurist

Cyrus McCormick (1809-1884), inventor of the reaper

Samuel F. B. Morse (1791-1872), inventor of the telegraph

Simon Newcomb (1835-1909), astronomer and mathematician

Eugene O'Neill (1888-1953), dramatist

Thomas Paine (1737-1809), political philosopher and author

Linus C. Pauling (1901-   ), scientist, educator

Robert E. Peary (1856-1920), explorer—discovered the North Pole

William Penn (1644-1718), colonizer

John J. Pershing (1860-1948), Commander of the American Expeditionary Forces in World War I

Edgar Allan Poe (1809-1849), poet and short story writer

William S. Porter (O. Henry) (1862-1910), story writer

Walter Reed (1851-1902), army surgeon—discovered the cause of yellow fever

John D. Rockefeller (1839-1937), capitalist and philanthropist
Jonas E. Salk (1914-   ), medical scientist—developed a vaccine for the prevention of poliomyelitis
Carl Sandburg (1878-1967), biographer and poet
William T. Sherman (1820-1891), Union army general during the Civil War
John Philip Sousa (1854-1932), composer
Harriet Beecher Stowe (1811-1896), author
Edward Teller (1908-   ), physicist —developed the H-bomb
Harold C. Urey (1895-   ), physicist
Lillian D. Wald (1867-1940), social worker—founder of the Henry Street Settlement in New York City
Booker T. Washington (1856-1915), educator and author
Daniel Webster (1782-1852), orator and statesman
George Westinghouse (1846-1914), inventor
James A. M. Whistler (1834-1903), artist and painter
Walt Whitman (1819-1892), poet
Eli Whitney (1765-1825), inventor of the cotton engine used to separate the seeds from the cotton
John Greenleaf Whittier (1807-1892), poet and editor
Orville Wright (1871-1948), with his brother *Wilbur* (1867-1912), invented the airplane

FLAG OF THE ALLIANCE
OCT. 14TH.
1779

Famous American Quotations

"Taxation without representation is tyranny!"
SLOGAN OF THE AMERICAN REVOLUTION

"Give me liberty or give me death."
PATRICK HENRY, 1775

"Stand your ground. Don't fire unless fired upon; but if they mean to have a war, let it begin here."
CAPTAIN JOHN PARKER, 1775

"Don't fire until you see the whites of their eyes."
COLONEL WILLIAM PRESCOTT, 1775

"We must all hang together, or assuredly we will all hang separately."
BENJAMIN FRANKLIN, 1776

"We hold these truths to be self-evident: That all men are created equal; that they are endowed by their Creator with certain unalienable rights; that among these are life, liberty and the pursuit of happiness."
THOMAS JEFFERSON, 1776

"I regret that I have but one life to lose for my country."
NATHAN HALE, 1776

"These are the times that try men's souls."
THOMAS PAINE, 1776

"I have not yet begun to fight."
CAPTAIN JOHN PAUL JONES, U.S.N., 1779

"To be prepared for war is one of the most effectual means of preserving peace."
GEORGE WASHINGTON, 1790

"It is our true policy to steer clear of permanent alliances with any portion of the foreign world."
GEORGE WASHINGTON, 1796

"Millions for defense, but not one cent for tribute."
CHARLES C. PINCKNEY, 1797

"First in war, first in peace, first in the hearts of his countrymen."
RICHARD HENRY LEE, 1799

"Don't give up the ship!"
COMMANDER JAMES LAWRENCE, U.S.N., 1813

"We have met the enemy and they are ours."
COMMODORE OLIVER H. PERRY, U.S.N., 1813

"Our Country, right or wrong."
STEPHEN DECATUR, 1816

"The American continents . . . are henceforth not to be considered as subjects for future colonization by any European powers."
JAMES MONROE, 1823

"Liberty and Union, now and forever, one and inseparable."
DANIEL WEBSTER, 1830

"Our federal union! It must and shall be preserved."
ANDREW JACKSON, 1830

"The Constitution of the United States was not made merely for the generation that then existed, but for posterity."
HENRY CLAY, 1850

"Go West, young man."
JOHN B. L. SOULE, 1851

"A house divided against itself cannot stand."
ABRAHAM LINCOLN, 1858

"Damn the torpedoes! Full speed ahead."
ADMIRAL DAVID FARRAGUT, 1864

"With malice toward none, with charity for all, with firmness in the right, as God gives us to see the right, let us strive to finish the work we are in."
ABRAHAM LINCOLN, 1865

"He serves his party best who serves his country best."
RUTHERFORD B. HAYES, 1877

"War is hell."
GENERAL WILLIAM T. SHERMAN, 1879

"Public office is a public trust."
GROVER CLEVELAND, 1884

"Cultivate the highest and best citizenship; for upon it rests the destiny of our government."
WILLIAM McKINLEY, 1897

"The world must be made safe for democracy."
WOODROW WILSON, 1917

"Lafayette, we are here!"
GENERAL JOHN PERSHING, 1917

"Here rests in honored glory an American soldier known but to God."
INSCRIPTION ON THE TOMB OF THE UNKNOWNS,
ARLINGTON NATIONAL CEMETERY

"The only thing we have to fear is fear itself."
FRANKLIN D. ROOSEVELT, 1933

"We must be the great arsenal of democracy."
FRANKLIN D. ROOSEVELT, 1940

"I shall return."
GENERAL DOUGLAS MACARTHUR, 1942

"Discrimination, like a disease, must be attacked wherever it appears."
HARRY S TRUMAN, 1946

"We will fight, if fight we must, to keep our freedom and to prevent justice from being destroyed."
HARRY S TRUMAN, 1951

"Let us never negotiate out of fear. But let us never fear to negotiate."
JOHN F. KENNEDY, 1961

"And so my fellow Americans, ask not what your country can do for you, ask what you can do for your country.
"My fellow citizens of the world: Ask not what America will do for you, but what together we can do for the freedom of man."
JOHN F. KENNEDY, 1961

"Peace is a journey of a thousand miles, and it must be taken one step at a time."
LYNDON B. JOHNSON, 1964

"Houston, Tranquility Base here. The Eagle has landed."
"That's one small step for man, one giant leap for mankind."
ASTRONAUT NEIL A. ARMSTRONG, 1969

"Proclaim liberty throughout all the land unto all the inhabitants thereof."
INSCRIPTION ON THE LIBERTY BELL, 1776

Growth of the United States
(In Order of Admission)
The Thirteen Original States

Connecticut	Massachusetts	Pennsylvania
Delaware	New Hampshire	Rhode Island
Georgia	New Jersey	South Carolina
Maryland	New York	Virginia
	North Carolina	

State	Date of Admission	State	Date of Admission
14. Vermont	1791	32. Minnesota	1858
15. Kentucky	1792	33. Oregon	1859
16. Tennessee	1796	34. Kansas	1861
17. Ohio	1803	35. West Virginia	1863
18. Louisiana	1812	36. Nevada	1864
19. Indiana	1816	37. Nebraska	1867
20. Mississippi	1817	38. Colorado	1876
21. Illinois	1818	39. North Dakota	1889
22. Alabama	1819	40. South Dakota	1889
23. Maine	1820	41. Montana	1889
24. Missouri	1821	42. Washington	1889
25. Arkansas	1836	43. Idaho	1890
26. Michigan	1837	44. Wyoming	1890
27. Florida	1845	45. Utah	1896
28. Texas	1845	46. Oklahoma	1907
29. Iowa	1846	47. New Mexico	1912
30. Wisconsin	1848	48. Arizona	1912
31. California	1850	49. Alaska	1959
		50. Hawaii	1959

The Fifty States

State	Abbreviation*		Nickname	Capital	Approximate Land Area (Sq. Mi.)
Alabama	Ala.	(AL)	Cotton State	Montgomery	51,100
Alaska	....	(AK)	....	Juneau	586,400
Arizona	Ariz.	(AZ)	Grand Canyon State	Phoenix	113,600
Arkansas	Ark.	(AR)	Land of Opportunity	Little Rock	52,700
California	Calif.	(CA)	Golden State	Sacramento	156,700

State	Abbreviation*		Nickname	Capital	Approximate Land Area (Sq. Mi.)
Colorado	Colo.	(CO)	Centennial State	Denver	104,000
Connecticut	Conn.	(CT)	Nutmeg State	Hartford	4,900
Delaware	Del.	(DE)	First State	Dover	2,000
Florida	Fla.	(FL)	Sunshine State	Tallahassee	54,300
Georgia	Ga.	(GA)	Peach State	Atlanta	58,500
Hawaii	....	(HI)	Aloha State	Honolulu	6,400
Idaho	....	(ID)	Gem State	Boise	82,800
Illinois	Ill.	(IL)	Prairie State	Springfield	55,900
Indiana	Ind.	(IN)	Hoosier State	Indianapolis	36,200
Iowa	....	(IA)	Hawkeye State	Des Moines	56,000
Kansas	Kans.	(KS)	Sunflower State	Topeka	82,100
Kentucky	Ky.	(KY)	Blue Grass State	Frankfort	39,900
Louisiana	La.	(LA)	Pelican State	Baton Rouge	45,200
Maine	....	(ME)	Pine Tree State	Augusta	31,000
Maryland	Md.	(MD)	Free State	Annapolis	9,900
Massachusetts	Mass.	(MA)	Bay State	Boston	7,900
Michigan	Mich.	(MI)	Wolverine State	Lansing	57,000
Minnesota	Minn.	(MN)	North Star State	St. Paul	80,000
Mississippi	Miss.	(MS)	Magnolia State	Jackson	47,200
Missouri	Mo.	(MO)	Show Me State	Jefferson City	69,200
Montana	Mont.	(MT)	Treasure State	Helena	145,900
Nebraska	Nebr.	(NB)	Beef State	Lincoln	76,700
Nevada	Nev.	(NV)	Silver State	Carson City	109,800
New Hampshire	N.H.	(NH)	Granite State	Concord	9,000
New Jersey	N.J.	(NJ)	Garden State	Trenton	7,500
New Mexico	N. Mex.	(NM)	Land of Enchantment	Santa Fe	121,500
New York	N.Y.	(NY)	Empire State	Albany	47,900
North Carolina	N.C.	(NC)	Tar Heel State	Raleigh	49,100
North Dakota	N. Dak.	(ND)	Sioux State	Bismarck	70,100
Ohio	....	(OH)	Buckeye State	Columbus	41,000
Oklahoma	Okla.	(OK)	Sooner State	Oklahoma City	69,000
Oregon	Oreg.	(OR)	Beaver State	Salem	96,300
Pennsylvania	Pa.	(PA)	Keystone State	Harrisburg	45,000
Rhode Island	R.I.	(RI)	Little Rhody	Providence	1,100
South Carolina	S.C.	(SC)	Palmetto State	Columbia	30,300
South Dakota	S. Dak.	(SD)	Cayote State	Pierre	76,600
Tennessee	Tenn.	(TN)	Volunteer State	Nashville	41,800
Texas	Tex.	(TX)	Lone Star State	Austin	263,500
Utah	....	(UT)	Beehive State	Salt Lake City	82,300
Vermont	Vt.	(VT)	Green Mountain State	Montpelier	9,300
Virginia	Va.	(VA)	Old Dominion	Richmond	39,900
Washington	Wash.	(WA)	Evergreen State	Olympia	66,800
West Virginia	W. Va.	(WV)	Mountain State	Charleston	24,100
Wisconsin	Wis.	(WI)	Badger State	Madison	54,700
Wyoming	Wyo.	(WY)	Equality State	Cheyenne	97,500

* Special 2-letter abbreviations authorized by the Post Office for use with ZIP code are noted in parentheses after the generally used abbreviations for the states, the District of Columbia and United States possessions.

Dependencies, Districts, Possessions, and Territories

American Samoa	.....		Pago Pago	76
Canal Zone	C.Z.	(CZ)	Balboa	650
District of Columbia	D.C.	(DC)	Washington	69
Guam	.....	(GU)	Agana	206
Puerto Rico	P.R.	(PR)	San Juan	3,400
(Commonwealth)				
Virgin Islands	V.I.	(VI)	St. Thomas	133

also Midway, Wake and several other small outposts in the Pacific Ocean

The Fifty Largest Cities in the United States

Rank	City	Population*
1	New York, NY	7,071,000
2	Chicago, IL	3,005,000
3	Los Angeles, CA	2,967,000
4	Philadelphia, PA	1,688,000
5	Houston, TX	1,594,000
6	Detroit, MI	1,203,000
7	Dallas, TX	904,000
8	San Diego, CA	876,000
9	Baltimore, MD	787,000
10	San Antonio, TX	785,000
11	Phoenix, AZ	765,000
12	Indianapolis, IN	701,000
13	San Francisco, CA	679,000
14	Memphis, TN	646,000
15	Washington, DC	638,000

Rank	City	Population*
16	San Jose, CA	637,000
17	Milwaukee, WI	636,000
18	Cleveland, OH	574,000
19	Columbus, OH	565,000
20	Boston, MA	563,000
21	New Orleans, LA	557,000
22	Jacksonville, FL	541,000
23	Seattle, WA	494,000
24	Denver, CO	491,000
25	Nashville, TN	456,000
26	St. Louis, MO	453,000
27	Kansas City, MO	448,000
28	El Paso, TX	425,000
29	Atlanta, GA	425,000
30	Pittsburgh, PA	424,000
31	Oklahoma City, OK	403,000
32	Cincinnati, OH	385,000
33	Fort Worth, TX	385,000
34	Minneapolis, MN	371,000
35	Portland, OR	366,000
36	Honolulu, HI	365,000
37	Long Beach, CA	361,000
38	Tulsa, OK	361,000
39	Buffalo, NY	358,000
40	Toledo, OH	355,000
41	Miami, FL	347,000
42	Austin, TX	345,000
43	Oakland, CA	339,000
44	Tucson, AZ	331,000
45	Albuquerque, NM	330,000
46	Newark, NJ	329,000
47	Charlotte, NC	314,000
48	Omaha, NB	312,000
49	Louisville, KY	298,000
50	Birmingham, AL	284,000

* Based on 1980 census figures

Holidays and Other Special Days

April Fool's Day, April 1
Pranksters feel that it is permissible to play all sorts of tricks on this day.

Ash Wednesday
The first day of Lent, generally in February or March.

Christmas Day, December 25
This is both a legal and religious holiday. It observes the anniversary of the birth of Jesus. All states and all those of the Christian faith celebrate this holiday.

Citizenship Day, September 17
This special day replaced I Am An American Day, formerly the third Sunday in May, and Constitution Day, September 17.

Columbus Day
The second Monday in October, to commemorate the discovery of America by Columbus in 1492. Prior to 1971, it was celebrated on October 12, the anniversary of the discovery. It is a legal holiday in many states.

Easter Sunday
The first Sunday after the first full moon that occurs at the end of the vernal equinox.

Election Day
The first Tuesday after the first Monday in November for the election of public officials. This holiday is observed in most states.

Father's Day
The third Sunday in June, set aside to honor fathers.

Flag Day, June 14
Public holiday observed in some states. Commemorates the adoption of the flag (Stars and Stripes) by the Continental Congress in 1777.

Good Friday
The Friday before Easter.

Halloween, October 31
A special day for making merry, wearing costumes and playing old-fashioned games. A favorite with children.

Independence Day, July 4
Legal holiday observed in all states. The Declaration of Independence was adopted on this day, in 1776.

Labor Day
The first Monday in September. Set aside to honor labor, it is a legal holiday in all states.

Lincoln's Birthday, February 12
Legal holiday in many states.

Martin Luther King's Birthday, January 15
This special day honoring a great civil rights leader is observed in many states.

Memorial Day
The last Monday in May, to honor the memory of the dead of all wars. Prior to 1971, it was celebrated on May 30. The observance of Memorial Day originated during the Civil War.

Mother's Day
The second Sunday in May, set aside to honor mothers.

New Year's Day, January 1
Legal holiday observed in all states.

Palm Sunday
The Sunday before Easter.

St. Patrick's Day, March 17
Observance of the death of Ireland's patron saint.

Thanksgiving Day
Generally the fourth Thursday in November, set aside for national thanksgiving, especially for our democratic form of government. It is a legal holiday in all states.

United Nations Day, October 24
This special day commemorates the founding of the United Nations in 1945.

Valentine's Day, February 14
Candy, flowers and other tokens of affection are exchanged on this day, in honor of two martyrs, both named St. Valentine.

Veterans' Day, November 11
Set aside to honor the veterans of the U.S. Armed Forces, it is a legal holiday in almost all states.

Washington's Birthday
The third Monday in February, in honor of the founder and first president of the United States. Prior to 1971, it was celebrated on February 22. It is a legal holiday in almost all states.

United States Currency

Coins:

Penny	one cent	1¢ or $.01
Nickel	five cents	5¢ or $.05
Dime	ten cents	10¢ or $.10
Quarter	twenty-five cents	25¢ or $.25
Half dollar	fifty cents	50¢ or $.50
Dollar	one dollar	$1 or $1.00

Bills:

		Portrait on Face of Bill
One dollar	$1	Washington
Two dollars	$2	Jefferson
Five dollars	$5	Lincoln
Ten dollars	$10	Hamilton
Twenty dollars	$20	Jackson
Fifty dollars	$50	Grant
One hundred dollars	$100	Franklin
Five hundred dollars	$500	McKinley
One thousand dollars	$1000	Cleveland
Five thousand dollars	$5000	Madison
Ten thousand dollars	$10,000	Chase

Currency may be expressed either in figures or spelled in words:

36¢	thirty-six cents
$.98	ninety-eight cents
$1.01	one dollar and one cent; a dollar and a cent
$1.10	one dollar and ten cents
$1.25	one dollar and twenty-five cents; a dollar and a quarter
$1.50	one dollar and fifty cents; a dollar and a half
$1.75	one dollar and seventy-five cents
$39.95	thirty-nine dollars and ninety-five cents
$142.58	one hundred forty-two dollars and fifty-eight cents
$1376.98	one thousand three hundred seventy-six dollars and ninety-eight cents; or thirteen hundred seventy-six dollars and ninety-eight cents
$19,463.58	nineteen thousand, four hundred sixty-three dollars and fifty-eight cents
$486,592.31	four hundred eighty-six thousand, five hundred ninety-two dollars and thirty-one cents
$1,025,416.38	one million, twenty-five thousand, four hundred sixteen dollars and thirty-eight cents

Cardinal Numbers

Typewritten symbols of the number series:

1   2   3   4   5   6   7   8   9   0

Handwritten symbols of the number series:

1   2   3   4   5   6   7   8   9   0

Cardinal numbers are used in counting to answer the question, "How many?" Numbers may be expressed either in figures or spelled out as words:

1 one	11 eleven	21 twenty-one	100 one hundred
2 two	12 twelve	25 twenty-five	or a hundred
3 three	13 thirteen	30 thirty	150 one hundred fifty
4 four	14 fourteen	35 thirty-five	200 two hundred
5 five	15 fifteen	40 forty	300 three hundred
6 six	16 sixteen	50 fifty	400 four hundred
7 seven	17 seventeen	60 sixty	500 five hundred
8 eight	18 eighteen	70 seventy	600 six hundred
9 nine	19 nineteen	80 eighty	700 seven hundred
10 ten	20 twenty	90 ninety	800 eight hundred
			900 nine hundred

1000	one thousand or a thousand
1500	one thousand five hundred or fifteen hundred
2000	two thousand
2500	two thousand five hundred or twenty-five hundred
3000	three thousand
5000	five thousand
10,000	ten thousand
10,500	ten thousand, five hundred
11,000	eleven thousand
15,000	fifteen thousand
20,000	twenty thousand
50,000	fifty thousand
100,000	one hundred thousand
150,000	one hundred fifty thousand
1,000,000	one million or a million
10,000,000	ten million
100,000,000	one hundred million or a hundred million
1,000,000,000	one billion or a billion
1,000,000,000,000	one trillion or a trillion

The number 14,653,897 is spelled out as follows:

fourteen million, six hundred fifty-three thousand, eight hundred ninety-seven

Ordinal Numbers

Ordinal numbers are used to show the order or position in a series. Like cardinal numbers, they may be expressed in figures or spelled out as words.

1st	first	11th	eleventh	21st	twenty first
2nd or 2d	second	12th	twelfth	25th	twenty-fifth
3rd	third	13th	thirteenth	30th	thirtieth
4th	fourth	14th	fourteenth	40th	fortieth
5th	fifth	15th	fifteenth	50th	fiftieth
6th	sixth	16th	sixteenth	60th	sixtieth
7th	seventh	17th	seventeenth	70th	seventieth
8th	eighth	18th	eighteenth	80th	eightieth
9th	ninth	19th	nineteenth	90th	ninetieth
10th	tenth	20th	twentieth	100th	one hundredth or a hundredth

150th	one hundred fiftieth
200th	two hundredth
300th	three hundredth
400th	four hundredth
500th	five hundredth
1000th	one thousandth
3000th	three thousandth
5000th	five thousandth
10,000th	ten thousandth
50,000th	fifty thousandth
100,000th	one hundred thousandth
1,000,000th	one millionth
100,000,000th	one hundred millionth
1,000,000,000th	one billionth

241st is spelled out as two hundred forty-first
365th is spelled out as three hundred sixty-fifth
1755th is spelled out as one thousand seven hundred fifty-fifth
45,608th is spelled out as forty-five thousand, six hundred eighth

Ordinal numbers, with the exception of *first* and *second*, are also used as denominators with spelled-out fractions. (Note that *half* is used instead of *second*.)

$\frac{1}{4}$ one-fourth; $\frac{2}{3}$ two-thirds; $\frac{5}{6}$ five-sixths; $\frac{1}{2}$ one-half
$\frac{1}{3}$ one-third; $\frac{4}{5}$ four-fifths; $\frac{3}{8}$ three-eighths

Roman Numerals

The letters used in forming Roman numerals are I, V, X, L, C, D and M. Capital letters are used except for pages of introduction in books. Periods are not required, as Roman numerals are not abbreviations.

1	I	11	XI	21	XXI	60	LX	400	CD
2	II	12	XII	22	XXII	70	LXX	500	D
3	III	13	XIII	23	XXIII	80	LXXX	600	DC
4	IV	14	XIV	24	XXIV	90	XC	900	CM
5	V	15	XV	25	XXV	100	C	1000	M
6	VI	16	XVI	30	XXX	150	CL	1500	MD
7	VII	17	XVII	35	XXXV	200	CC	2000	MM
8	VIII	18	XVIII	40	XL	250	CCL	3000	MMM
9	IX	19	XIX	45	XLV	300	CCC	4000	$M\overline{V}$
10	X	20	XX	50	L	350	CCCL	5000	$\overline{V}$

Rules for forming Roman Numerals

1. A double letter doubles the value of a single letter; a triple letter triples the value of a single letter.

Example: I = 1 II = 2 III = 3 X = 10 XX = 20 XXX = 30
C = 100 CC = 200 CCC = 300
M = 1000 MM = 2000 MMM = 3000

2. A letter occurring after one of greater value is added to the one of greater value.

Example: VI = 6 XV = 15 LX = 60 CX = 110
DC = 600 MM = 1100 MD = 1500 $\overline{V}$M = 6000

3. A letter occurring before one of greater value is subtracted from the one of greater value.

Example: IV = 4 IX = 9 XL = 40 XC = 90
CD = 400 CM = 900 $M\overline{V}$ = 4000

4. Any number of thousands is shown by drawing a line over any numeral less than one thousand.

Example: $\overline{V}$ = 5000 $\overline{V}$MM = 7000 $\overline{X}$ = 10,000 $\overline{C}$ = 100,000

5. Any number of millions is shown by drawing a line over the 1000 numeral or any numeral more than one thousand.

Example: $\overline{\overline{M}}$ = one million $\overline{\overline{MM}}$ = two million

Weights, Measures and Counting Units
United States Customary System
Avoirdupois Weight

(Used for weighing all articles except drugs, precious metals and precious stones)

$27^{11}/_{32}$ grains = 1 dram
16 drams = 1 ounce
16 ounces = 1 pound = 256 drams
100 pounds = 1 hundredweight
2000 pounds = 1 ton (short ton)
2240 pounds = 1 long ton

Ordinary Liquid Measure

4 gills = 1 pint = 16 ounces
2 pints = 1 quart
4 quarts = 1 gallon
5 fifths = 1 gallon
7.48 gallons = 1 cubic foot
1 Imperial pint = 20 ounces
1 Imperial quart = 2 Imperial pints
1 Imperial gallon = 4 Imperial quarts

Linear Measure

12 inches = 1 foot
3 feet = 1 yard
5280 feet = 1 mile
1760 yards = 1 mile

Square Measure

144 square inches = 1 square foot
9 square feet = 1 square yard = 1296 square inches
43,560 square feet = 1 acre = 4840 square yards
640 acres = 1 square mile

Cubic Measure

1728 cubic inches = 1 cubic foot
27 cubic feet = 1 cubic yard

Circular Measure

60 seconds = 1 minute
60 minutes = 1 degree
90 degrees = 1 quadrant
360 degrees = 1 circle

Units of Time

60 seconds = 1 minute
60 minutes = 1 hour
24 hours = 1 day
7 days = 1 week
2 weeks = 1 fortnight
12 months = 1 year
365 days = 1 year (366 days in leap year)
10 years = 1 decade
100 years = 1 century

Counting Units

12 units = 1 dozen
12 dozen = 1 gross
20 units = 1 score

International Metric System

Commonly used units basic to the International Metric System are:

Weight—gram
Length—meter
Time—second

The following prefixes, combined with the basic unit names, provide the multiples and submultiples in the metric system:

Prefix	Equivalent	Prefix	Equivalent
mega	millionfold	deci	tenth part
kilo	thousandfold	centi	hundredth part
hecto	hundredfold	milli	thousandth part
deka	tenfold	micro	millionth part

Examples:

One kilogram = 1000 grams
One centimeter = 1/100 meter

Weight

10 milligrams	= 1 centigram		
10 centigrams	= 1 decigram	=	100 milligrams
10 decigrams	= 1 gram	=	1000 milligrams
10 grams	= 1 dekagram		
10 dekagrams	= 1 hectogram	=	100 grams
10 hectograms	= 1 kilogram	=	1000 grams
1000 kilograms	= 1 metric ton		

Volume Measure

10 milliliters   = 1 centiliter
10 centiliters   = 1 deciliter   =   100 milliliters
10 deciliters   = 1 liter   = 1000 milliliters
10 liters   = 1 dekaliter
10 dekaliters   = 1 hectoliter   =   100 liters
10 hectoliters   = 1 kiloliter   = 1000 liters

Linear Measure

10 millimeters   = 1 centimeter
10 centimeters   = 1 decimeter   =   100 millimeters
10 decimeters   = 1 meter   = 1000 millimeters
10 meters   = 1 dekameter
10 dekameters   = 1 hectometer   =   100 meters
10 hectometers   = 1 kilometer   = 1000 meters

Square (Area) Measure

100 square millimeters = 1 square centimeter
10,000 square centimeters = 1 square meter   = 1,000,000 square millimeters

100 square meters   = 1 are
100 ares   = 1 hectare   = 10,000 square meters
100 hectares   = 1 square kilometer   = 1,000,000 square meters

Cubic Measure

1000 cubic millimeters = 1 cubic centimeter
1000 cubic centimeters = 1 cubic decimeter   = 1,000,000 square meters
1000 cubic decimeters = 1 cubic meter   = 1,000,000 cubic centimeters

Table of Equivalents
Weight

1 ounce	28.35 grams	1 gram	0.04 ounce
1 pound	453.95 grams	1 kilogram	2.20 pounds
1 ton-short	0.91 metric ton	1 metric ton	2205 pounds
1 ton-long	1.02 metric tons		

Liquid Volume

1 ounce ⎰ 1.81 cubic inches
⎱ 29.57 milliliters   1 liter ⎰ 1.06 quarts
⎱ 61.02 cubic inches

1 pint ⎰ 28.88 cubic inches
⎱ 0.47 liter

1 quart ⎰ 57.75 cubic inches
⎱ 0.95 liter

1 gallon ⎰ 231 cubic inches
⎱ 3.79 liters

Linear Measure

1 inch	2.54 centimeters	1 millimeter	0.04 inch
1 foot	0.30 meter	1 centimeter	0.39 inch
1 yard	0.91 meter	1 kilometer	0.62 mile
1 mile	1.61 kilometers	1 meter	39.37 inches

Area or Surface

1 square inch	6.45 square centimeters	1 square millimeter	0.002 square inch
1 square foot	929.03 square centimeters	1 square centimeter	0.16 square inch
1 square yard	0.84 square meter	1 square kilometer	0.39 square mile
1 square mile	259.00 hectares	1 square meter	10.76 square feet

Volume (Cubic)

1 cubic inch	16.39 cubic centimeters	1 cubic centimeter	0.06 cubic inch
1 cubic foot	28.32 cubic decimeters	1 cubic meter	1.31 cubic yards

The Lincoln mourning flag of 36 stars emphasizes geometric precision in the placement of its stars in the shape of a pentagram. A band of crepe was sewn around the border when President Lincoln was assassinated in 1865.

General Information

Did the United States ever have an "open-admission" policy to encourage immigration to this country?

Yes. During this country's first hundred years, there were no federal laws restricting the admission of aliens to the United States. The need for settlers was very great and all immigrants were welcomed.

What restrictions were first placed on the admission of aliens?

In 1875, the first federal law was enacted to bar convicts and other undesirables. Additional grounds for exclusion were added later.

At one time, Chinese, Japanese and other Asians were also barred. However, such exclusion was repealed in the 1940's and 1950's.

When were restrictions limiting the number of immigrants adopted?

In 1924, restrictions based on a system of quotas for each country keyed to "national origins" of the population of the United States were adopted. These quotas favored immigration from Northern and Western European countries.

What were the objections to the old "national origins" quota system which was used until 1965 to control the number of immigrants admitted to this country?

Under the "national origins" quota system, the number of people allowed to enter this country was apportioned according to the ethnic composition of the United States as of 1920. This system discriminated against Southern and Eastern Europeans as well as Asians, and provided the highest quotas to those countries that had the least need for emigration.

Does the admission of all aliens to the United States depend on quotas based on the immigrants' place of birth?

No. The Immigration and Nationalization Act, as amended through 1981, provides one worldwide quota system, with a per country limit of 20,000 people a year and preferences based on job skills and relationship to U.S. citizens or lawful permanent residents. The total number of immigrants admitted under the preference system is 270,000 per year. Certain categories, such as immediate relatives of U.S. citizens and religious ministers, are exempt from the quota system, as are 50,000 refugees, or more under certain conditions.

First Look at the New World
1900-1920

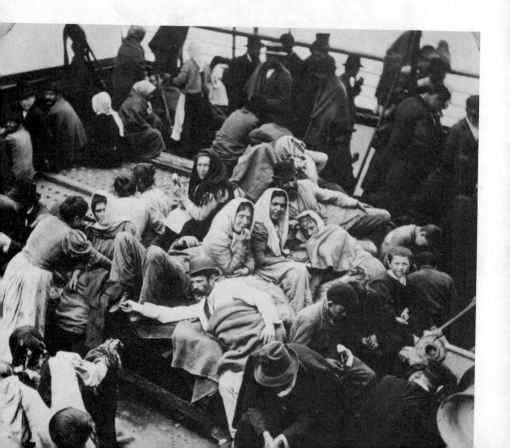

Waiting at Ellis Island

Medical Examinations

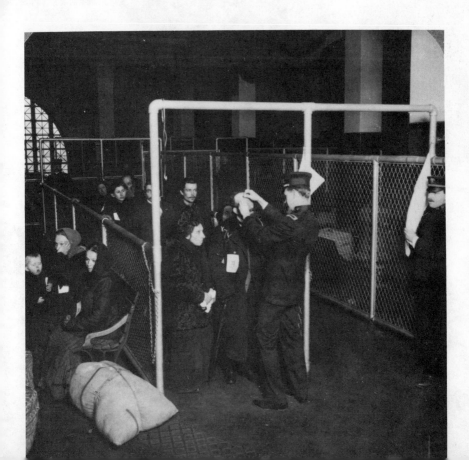

Citizenship Class

How does an alien who is abroad and wishes to come to the United States apply for a visa?

An alien who is not exempt from the visa requirement must apply to a U.S. Consular Officer abroad for a visa appropriate for the purpose for which entry is desired. Under certain circumstances, the U.S. Consular Officer can issue the visa immediately. Under other circumstances, the visa must be initiated through the U.S. Department of Labor or the Immigration and Naturalization Service.

Are all aliens who have the necessary legal documents admitted upon arrival in the U.S.?

No. Upon arrival at the United States port of entry, all aliens are again examined to determine if they should be admitted under the immigration laws.

Special Information for Nonimmigrants

What is meant by a "nonimmigrant"?

An alien applying for admission to the United States is classified as a "non-immigrant" if he or she belongs in any one of the following groups.

1. A foreign ambassador, public minister or diplomatic or consular officer and members of the immediate family and household (A)
2. An alien visiting the United States temporarily for business or pleasure (B-1, B-2)
3. An alien in transit through the United States (C-1), or an alien qualified to pass in transit to and from the United Nations Headquarters District and foreign countries (C-2)
4. An alien crewman who intends to land temporarily and solely in pursuit of employment as a crewman and then depart from the United States (D)
5. An alien entering the United States solely to carry on substantial trade between the United States and the foreign state of which he or she is a national (E-1); or to solely develop and direct the operations of an enterprise in which he or she has invested a substantial amount of capital, provided there exists certain treaty provisions between the United States and the country of which the alien is a national (E-2). The spouse and unmarried children under 21 years of age may accompany or follow to join the alien
6. A foreign student entering the United States temporarily to pursue a full course of study in an approved college,

university, seminary, conservatory, academic high school, elementary school or other academic institution, or in a language training program, and the alien spouse and minor children of such student (F)

7. A foreign representative to the United Nations or other international organization, or any officer or employee of an international organization, as well as members of the immediate family and household (G)

8. An alien of distinguished merit and ability coming temporarily to the United States to perform services of an exceptional nature (H-1), or an alien coming temporarily to perform other labor or services of a temporary nature in an area where there is a shortage of persons qualified to perform such labor or services (H-2), or an alien coming temporarily to the United States as an industrial trainee (H-3)

9. An accredited representative of the foreign press, radio, film or other information media entering the United States solely to engage in such work, and the spouse and unmarried children under 21 years of age (I)

10. An exchange visitor who is a foreign student, scholar, trainee, teacher, professor, research assistant, specialist or leader in a field of specialized knowledge or skill entering the United States temporarily as a participant in a program designated by the secretary of state, and the alien spouse and minor children (J)

11. An alien engaged to a U.S. citizen who seeks to enter the United States to marry the U.S. citizen within 90 days after entry, and such alien's unmarried minor children (K)

12. An intracompany transferee who is transferred to the United States by his employer to continue to render service to it or its affiliate in a managerial, executive or specialist capacity, provided the transferee has been employed abroad by that employer for at least one year. The alien spouse and unmarried minor children may accompany or follow to join the transferee (L)

13. A foreign student entering the United States temporarily to pursue a full course of study in an approved vocational or other recognized nonacademic institution (other than in a language training program), and the alien spouse and minor children of such student (M)

What must an alien abroad do in order to obtain a nonimmigrant visa for admission to the United States?

Most nonimmigrant visas require only an application to the American Consulate in the country where the alien resides. Necessary forms are supplied by the Consular Officer who advises the alien regarding the procedure to be followed. If the applicant is found to be qualified, the Consular Officer will issue a visa.

Is additional approval required for certain types of nonimmigrant visas?

Yes. Prior approval of visa petitions is required for the various alien groups coming for temporary employment in the United States, and for aliens engaged to marry American citizens (H-1, 2, 3; K; L).

Can nonimmigrants remain permanently in the United States?

No. Nonimmigrants are generally admitted for only a temporary stay in the United States. They must leave the United States when they have accomplished the purpose for which they were admitted or when the time for which they were admitted expires.

What happens if a nonimmigrant fails to leave the United States when he or she has accomplished the purpose for which admitted or when the time for which he or she was admitted expires?

Unless the nonimmigrant obtains an extension from the Immigration and Naturalization Service, he or she is subject to deportation.

Extension of Temporary Stay

Are there special provisions for extending the temporary stay of nonimmigrants in the United States?

Yes. Application may be made by most nonimmigrants to extend the time of temporary stay in the United States.

Are all nonimmigrants eligible for extension of their temporary stay in the United States?

No. An alien admitted in transit, a crewman, or a fiancé(e) and his or her children are ineligible for an extension of temporary stay.

Is a special form used by nonimmigrants wishing to apply for an extension of their temporary stay in the United States?

Yes. Most nonimmigrants admitted for a temporary period of time must apply for an extension of temporary stay in the United States by completing and submitting *Form I-539, Application to Extend Time of Temporary Stay*. Different special forms are used by student aliens (F), exchange aliens (J) and certain other nonimmigrants.

When should *Form I-539* be submitted?
Applications for extension of temporary stay should be submitted not less than 15 days nor more than 60 days before the authorized stay expires.

Where should *Form I-539* be submitted?
The completed application should be taken or mailed* to the office of the Immigration and Naturalization Service having jurisdiction over the place where the applicant is staying.

Is a fee required for filing *Form I-539?*
In almost all cases, a $5 fee must be paid for filing the application.

Change of Nonimmigrant Status

Can a lawfully admitted nonimmigrant who has not violated his or her status change to a new nonimmigrant classification?
Yes. Common examples are: a visitor for pleasure who, after entry, decides to remain in the United States to study; or a visitor for pleasure who, after entry, decides to remain as a visitor for business reasons.

Are all nonimmigrants eligible for change of their nonimmigrant status?
No. An alien admitted in transit, a crewman, some exchange visitors admitted in order to receive graduate medical education or training, or a fiancé(e) and his or her children are ineligible for change of nonimmigrant status.

What official form is used by the nonimmigrant to change to a new nonimmigrant classification?
Application for Change of Nonimmigrant Status, Form I-506 is used.

Are there special instructions that are a part of *Form I-506?*
Yes, there are instructions which must be read carefully. These instructions contain information on filing fee, supporting documents that must be submitted with the application and other pertinent information.

---

* When mailing applications or supporting documents, it is always advisable to send them by *certified mail, return receipt requested.*

Where is the *Form I-506* application submitted?
The completed application and supporting documents should be taken or mailed to the nearest office of the Immigration and Naturalization Service.

Documentation and Registration of Nonimmigrants

What is an *I-94* form?
Form I-94, Arrival-Departure Record, is a small (3" by 5") white paper completed by nonimmigrant aliens at the time of entry into the United States.

What purpose does the *I-94* form serve?
Form I-94 serves as a control document, entry-departure record and identification card.

Are nonimmigrants required to have an *I-94* form in their possession at all times?
Every nonimmigrant over the age of 18 is required to have the *I-94* form available at all times to show to an immigration officer, if so requested.

If a nonimmigrant loses his or her *I-94* form, can a duplicate be obtained?
Yes. The nonimmigrant alien may apply for a duplicate by submitting an application on *Form I-102, Application by Nonimmigrant Alien for Replacement of Arrival Document (I-94).* There is a $5 filing fee.

When the nonimmigrant leaves the United States after completing his or her temporary stay, what happens to the *I-94* form?
Upon departure of the alien from the United States, the *I-94* form must be surrendered to the steamship or airline company to serve as a record of departure.

Must nonimmigrants register with the Immigration and Naturalization Service annually?
No. However, most nonimmigrants must notify the Immigration and Naturalization Service on *Form AR-11* of any change in address within 10 days following the date on which the address was changed.

What group of nonimmigrants is exempted from this registration requirement?

Those who are exempted from alien registration are nonimmigrants who are accredited government officials, representatives of accredited international organizations, and members of their families and staffs.

Where may official forms be obtained for submitting the address reports?

Official forms for submitting the address reports are available at post offices or at any office of the Immigration and Naturalization Service.

Special Information for Immigrants

Categories and Preferences

What is meant by an *immigrant*?

According to the United States immigration laws, an immigrant is any alien applying for admission to the United States who is not a member of the nonimmigrant groups listed previously.

Are immigrants divided into different categories?

Yes, immigrants are divided into the following four categories:

1. Aliens who fall within one of the preference categories or in the nonpreference category
2. Special immigrants
3. Immediate relatives
4. Refugees

1. Aliens who fall within one of the preference categories or in the nonpreference category

What are the numerical restrictions for this group of aliens?

The entry of aliens in this group is restricted to 270,000 in any one year and to 20,000 for the natives of any one country.

What system is used for issuing visas to aliens in this group?

Aliens in this group are eligible for visas based upon the following preference system.

1st Preference—20 percent are available to qualified immigrants who are unmarried sons or daughters of American citizens.

2nd Preference—26 percent plus any not required for 1st preference are next available to qualified immigrants who are the spouses and unmarried sons or daughters or permanent resident aliens.

3rd Preference—10 percent are next available to qualified immigrants who are members of the professions or are of exceptional ability in the arts or sciences and whose skills are sought by a U.S. employer.

4th Preference—10 percent plus any not required for the first three preferences are next available to qualified immigrants who are the married sons or daughters of American citizens.

5th Preference—24 percent plus any not required by the first four preferences are next available to qualified immigrants who are the brothers or sisters of American citizens who are at least 21 years of age.

6th Preference—10 percent are next available to qualified immigrants capable of performing specified skilled or unskilled labor, not of a temporary or seasonal nature, for which there is a shortage of employable persons in the United States.

Nonpreference—Numbers which are not used in any of the previous categories are available to qualified nonpreference immigrants in the chronological order in which they qualify. There are presently no such numbers nor are there expected to be any in the foreseeable future.

Alien Labor Certification

What is meant by a *labor certification?*

A labor certification is a certification by the U.S. Department of Labor that there are not sufficient American citizens or permanent resident aliens who are able, willing, qualified and available to do the work the alien intends to do, and that the employment of the alien will not adversely affect the working conditions of persons similarly employed in the United States.

Is this certification required of all aliens seeking to enter the United States as permanent residents?

Yes, except for those aliens seeking permanent residence who can qualify under the family preferences, as an immediate relative or as a special immigrant.

How does an alien who wishes to enter the United States as a 3rd or 6th preference immigrant, or as a nonpreference immigrant obtain an alien employment certification?

Application for *Alien Employment Certification, Form ETA-750,* may be filed by a prospective employer on behalf of the alien with the local office of the State Labor Department. If the occupation is listed in the regulations of the U.S. Department of Labor as a Schedule A occupation, the application may be made directly with the Immigration and Naturalization Service, together with *Form I-140.*

What is a Schedule A occupation?

Schedule A is a list of occupations for which the Employment and Training Administration of the U.S. Department of Labor has already determined that there are not sufficient United States workers who are able, willing, qualified and available, and that the wages and working conditions of United States workers similarly employed will not be adversely affected by the employment of aliens.

Must aliens qualified in such occupations apply for an alien labor certification?

No. Such aliens are considered "precertified" and may make application for preference classification directly to the Immigration and Naturalization Service.

What occupations are currently listed in Schedule A?

Occupations currently listed in Schedule A are:

(a) Group 1:
(1) Persons who will be employed as physical therapists, and who possess all the qualifications necessary to take the physical therapist licensing examination in the state in which they propose to practice physical therapy.
(2) Alien graduates of foreign medical schools who will be employed as physicians (or surgeons) in a geographic area which has been designated by the Secretary of Department of Health and Human Services (HHS) as a Health Manpower Shortage Area for the alien's medical specialty, or has been identified otherwise by the Secretary of HHS as having an insufficient number of physicians in the alien's medical specialty . . .

(3) Aliens who will be employed as professional nurses; and (i) who have passed the Commission on Graduates of Foreign Nursing Schools (CGFNS) Examination; or (ii) who hold a full and unrestricted license to practice professional nursing in the state of intended employment . . .

(b) Group II:

Aliens (except for aliens in the performing arts) of exceptional ability in the sciences or arts including college and university teachers of exceptional ability who have been practicing their science or art during the year prior to application and who intend to practice the same science or art in the United States . . . An alien, however, need not have studied at a college or university in order to qualify for the Group II occupation.

(c) Group III:

(1) Aliens who seek admission to the United States in order to perform a religious occupation, such as the preaching or teaching of religion; and

(2) Aliens with a religious commitment who seek admission into the United States in order to work for a nonprofit religious organization.

(d) Group IV:

(1) Aliens who have been admitted to the United States in order to work in, and who are currently working in, managerial or executive positions with the same international corporations or organizations with which they were continuously employed as managers or executives outside the United States for one year before they were admitted.

(2) Aliens outside the United States who will be engaged in the United States in managerial or executive positions with the same international corporations or organizations with which they have been continuously employed as managers or executives outside the United States for the immediately prior year.

2. Special immigrants

What are the different kinds of "special immigrants"?

The following are the different kinds of "special immigrants":

a. An immigrant lawfully admitted for permanent residence who is returning from a temporary visit abroad

b. An immigrant who was an American citizen and wishes to reacquire citizenship

c. A minister, as well as spouse and unmarried minor children, provided that he or she has been a practicing minister for at least two years immediately preceding the time of application for admission, that the minister seeks to enter solely for the purpose of carrying on his or her vocation, and that such services are needed by an accredited religious denomination

d. An employee or a retired former employee of the United States Government abroad who has served for 15 years or more, and accompanying spouse and unmarried minor children, provided the secretary of state finds it in the national interest to approve the granting of a special immigrant status.

Are there any numerical restrictions for these different kinds of special immigrants?

No. All special immigrants may be admitted to the United States without any numerical limitation.

3. Immediate relatives

What is meant by the term *immediate relatives*?

This term means unmarried children under 21 years of age, spouses and parents of American citizens. In the case of parents, however, the American citizen must be at least 21 years of age.

Are there any numerical limitations for this group of aliens?

No. Immediate relatives are admitted to the United States without any numerical limitation.

4. Refugees

What is meant by *refugees*?

The Refugee Act of 1979 defines *refugees* as aliens who are unwilling or unable to return to their country because of persecution or a well-founded fear of persecution on account of race, religion, nationality, membership in a particular social group, or political opinion.

Why is the Refugee Act of 1979 important?

This act established the first comprehensive United States refugee settlement and assistance program, sought to correct inadequate laws regarding the treatment and admission of refugees to the United States, and broadened the definition of *refugee*. The act—

a. raised the annual limitation on regular refugee admissions to 50,000;

b. provided a new definition of *refugee* that recognized the plight of homeless people all over the world;

c. provided an orderly but flexible procedure to meet emergency refugee situations if the resettlement needs of the homeless people involved could not be met within the annual limitation of 50,000 refugees;

d. provided for federal support of the refugee resettlement process.

What is meant by "granting asylum"?

Granting asylum is providing refuge in the United States to persons who have fled other countries to escape persecution.

Has the United States been a haven for refugees?

Yes. The United States has been a haven for many persons fleeing from religious and political persecution. Since World War II, millions of refugees have been admitted into the United States.

Where have these refugees come from?

Asylum has been granted refugees from Eastern and Central Europe, the Soviet Union, the Middle East, Central America, Hong Kong, Vietnam, Cambodia, Thailand and Indonesia, as well as other parts of the world.

Can an alien who is physically present in the United States or is at a land border or port of entry apply for asylum?

Yes, a procedure for such application has been established by the attorney general, who may grant asylum if it is determined that the alien qualifies as a refugee.

Can such asylum be terminated?

Yes, it may be terminated by the Attorney General if the alien no longer qualifies as an asylee.

Can refugees or asylees adjust their status to that of lawful permanent residents?

Yes. Any alien whose admission as a refugee or asylee has not been terminated by the attorney general and who has been physically present in the United States for at least one year may, after examination by the Immigration and Naturalization Service, be regarded as lawfully admitted for permanent residence as of the date of such alien's arrival in the United States.

Entry Documents

What must aliens living abroad do in order to obtain an immigrant visa?

Applications for an immigrant visa are generally made to the American Consulate in the country where the alien resides. Necessary forms are supplied by the Consular Officer who advises the alien regarding the procedure to be followed.

Who issues immigrant visas?

Immigrant visas are issued by the United States Consular Officers abroad.

What must an alien ordinarily present in order to obtain an immigrant visa?

An alien must ordinarily present a passport showing his or her origin, identity and nationality.

Is prior approval necessary before certain immigrant visas are issued?

Yes, certain immigrant visas are issued only if petitions for their issuance have been approved in advance by the Immigration and Naturalization Service.

What immigrant visas require prior approval by the Immigration and Naturalization Service?

Petitions for the issuance of the following visas must be approved in advance:

1. A preference immigrant visa
2. An immigrant visa for an "immediate relative"

Is a fee required for an immigrant visa?

Yes. The required fee in connection with the issuance of an immigrant visa is $25.

For how long is an immigrant visa valid?

The immigrant visa is generally valid for four months from the date of issuance. Immigrants lawfully entering the United States within the four months are admitted for permanent residence.

If an alien meets the eligibility requirements for an immigrant visa, does he or she have the right to receive a visa and automatically enter the United States?

No. Although an alien may meet the eligibility requirements for an immigrant visa, the alien may be denied a visa by an American Consul abroad or be denied admission to the United States at the port of entry by the Immigration and Naturalization Service if found to be excludable on grounds specified in the immigration laws.

What are the grounds upon which aliens may be found to be excludable?

Some of the grounds for excluding aliens from admission into the United States are that—

1. they are not mentally sound or physically fit;
2. they are narcotic drug addicts or chronic alcoholics;
3. they are paupers, professional beggars or vagrants;
4. they are criminals;
5. they are polygamists;
6. they are afflicted with a dangerous contagious disease;
7. they are prostitutes, have engaged in prostitution or are coming to the United States to engage in unlawful commercialized vice;
8. they are over 16 years of age and cannot read or understand some language or dialect;
9. they have improper or fraudulent documents;
10. they have previously been deported;
11. they are members of the Communist or other totalitarian party;
12. under the direction of, or in association with the Nazi government, they participated in the persecution of any person because of race, religion, national origin or political opinion;
13. their entry would be prejudicial to the public interest or would endanger the welfare or security of the United States.

Visa Petitions

In order to qualify for preference consideration under the Immigration and Nationality Act, what visa petitions must be submitted?

All preference categories are petitioned for on either *Form I-130* or *Form I-140*. Form I-130 is used to establish a preference based on a family relationship to a United States citizen or a lawfully admitted permanent resident; this form is also used to establish classification as an immediate relative of a United States citizen. *Form I-140* is used to establish a preference for immigration based on an alien's job skills or occupation, after a labor certification has been obtained.

Does approval of a visa petition assure that the alien will be found eligible for visa issuance, admission to the United States, or adjustment of lawful permanent residence?

No, approval of a visa petition merely gives the alien an appropriate classification. It is just the first step toward qualifying for permanent residence in the United States.

What is the name of *Form I-130*?

Form I-130 is called a *Petition to Classify Status of Alien Relative for Issuance of Immigrant Visa.*

By whom is the *Form I-130* petition generally filed?

The petition is generally filed by a citizen or a lawful permanent resident of the United States to classify the status of alien relatives.

Is there a fee required for filing *Form I-130*?

Yes, a fee of $10 must be paid for filing this petition.

Where is the *Form I-130* petition submitted?

If the petitioner resides in the United States, he or she sends the completed petition to the office of the Immigration and Naturalization Service closest to his or her place of residence. If residing abroad, the petitioner should consult the nearest American Consulate as to the consular office designated to act on the petition.

Are there special instructions that are a part of *Form I-130*?

Yes, there are such instructions which should be read carefully. These instructions specify eligibility requirements and supporting documents that must be submitted with the petition. They contain information on how to prepare the petition, and other pertinent information.

What is the name of *Form I-140*?

Form I-140 is called a *Petition to Classify Preference of Alien on Basis of Profession or Occupation.*

Who may file a *Form I-140* petition?

Once a labor certification is obtained, a petition to grant an alien a 3rd preference classification may be filed by the alien or by the employer in the alien's behalf. The alien must be a member of the professions or a person who because of exceptional ability in the sciences or arts will substantially benefit the national economy, cultural interests or welfare of the United States, and whose services are sought by an American employer.

A petition to grant an alien a 6th preference classification may be filed only by an employer desiring and intending to employ within the United States an alien who is capable of performing specified skilled or unskilled labor, not of a temporary or seasonal nature, for which the U.S. Department of Labor has issued a certification that there is a shortage of employable and willing persons existing in the area of intended employment.

Is there a fee required for filing *Form I-140?*
Yes, a fee of $25 must be paid for filing this petition.

Where is the *Form I-140* petition submitted?
A person signing the petition outside the United States must take the completed petition to an American Consular Officer who will administer the oath of confirmation and furnish the address of the office of the Immigration and Naturalization Service in the United States to which the petition should be sent by the petitioner.

A person executing the petition in the United States must take or mail the completed petition to the office of the Immigration and Naturalization Service having jurisdiction over the intended place of employment.

Are there special instructions that are a part of *Form I-140?*
Yes, there are such instructions which should be read carefully. These instructions contain information on supporting documents that must be submitted with the petition, oath required, and other pertinent information.

Affidavit of Support

What is an *Affidavit of Support?*
Affidavit of Support, Form I-134 is used by a sponsor to indicate to the Immigration and Naturalization Service or to a Consular Officer that the sponsor will be responsible for the financial maintenance of the alien.

Why is *Form I-134* an important immigration document?
In connection with an application for an immigrant visa or adjustment of status based on an alien's relationship to a United States citizen or a lawful permanent resident, proof may be required that the alien will not become a public charge. *Form I-134* is used to provide such proof.

When is *Form I-134* used?

Generally, all applications based on family relationship should be accompanied by *Form I-134*.

Occasionally, an American Consul may request a *Form I-134* in connection with an application for a nonimmigrant visa such as an F-1 (student) visa or a B-2 (tourist) visa.

Waiver of Entry Documents

Are all immigrants required to present either a visa or a passport?

No. The following are not required to present a visa or a passport.

1. A lawful permanent resident of the United States returning from a temporary absence abroad, who—
   a. was absent for not more than one year and possesses an alien registration receipt card *(Form I-151 or I-551)*, or
   b. possesses a valid unexpired reentry permit, or
   c. is the spouse or child of a member of the Armed Forces of the United States stationed abroad
2. A child born during the temporary visit abroad of a mother who is a lawful permanent resident alien or a national of the United States
3. A child born subsequent to the issuance of an immigrant visa to an accompanying parent who applies for admission and possesses a valid unexpired visa.

Are any immigrants required to present visas but not passports?

The following are required to present visas but not passports.

1. An alien who has been lawfully admitted to the United States for permanent residence, who is returning after a temporary absence
2. An immigrant who is stateless or who, because of opposition to communism, is unable or unwilling to obtain a passport from the country of nationality, or is the accompanying spouse or unmarried son or daughter of such immigrant
3. An immigrant who is the parent, spouse or unmarried son or daughter of an American citizen or an alien lawfully admitted to the United States for permanent residence
4. An immigrant who is a member of the Armed Forces of the United States traveling on military orders
5. An alien who is a 3rd preference immigrant.

Evidence of Admission to Lawful Permanent Residence (Green Card)

What is a "green card"?

The "green card," now a beige card *(Form I-551)*, is official evidence that an alien has become a permanent resident of the United States. The alien obtains this status by qualifying for one of the permanent visa categories mentioned earlier.

Must the "green card" be carried at all times by permanent residents?

All permanent residents over 18 years of age must carry their "green card."

What must an alien do if he or she loses the "green card"?

A lost "green card" may be replaced by filing *Form I-90* in person, together with proper photographs and a $15 fee, at the nearest office of the Immigration and Naturalization Service, if the alien is in the United States. If outside the United States, the alien must file at the nearest U.S. Consulate.

Immigrant Registration

Are immigrants required to notify the Immigration and Naturalization Service periodically of their current address?

Annual notification is no longer required. However, all immigrants must notify the Immigration and Naturalization Service on *Form AR-11* of any change in address within 10 days following the date on which the address was changed.

Where may official forms be obtained for submitting the address reports?

Official forms for submitting the address reports are available at post offices or at any office of the Immigration and Naturalization Service.

Reentry Documents

What is a reentry permit?
A reentry permit is issued to an alien going abroad temporarily after being admitted to the United States for permanent residence.

What is the advantage of having a reentry permit when traveling abroad?
The possession of a reentry permit makes it possible for an alien to apply for readmission to the United States without having to obtain a new immigrant visa.

When must an application for a reentry permit be filed?
It must be filed by the alien at least 30 days before the proposed departure.

For how long is a reentry permit valid?
A reentry permit is valid for not more than two years from the date of issuance. No extensions or renewals are permitted.

Is a special form used to apply for a reentry permit?
Yes. *Form I-131, Application for Issuance of Permit to Reenter the United States* is the form used for such application.

Change in Status to Permanent Resident

Can nonimmigrant aliens apply for a change of status to permanent resident aliens?
Yes.

Can the adjustment in status to permanent resident alien be made without leaving the United States?
In many cases, yes. Present immigration law permits an alien to apply for adjustment of his or her status without leaving the United States, under the following conditions:

1. The applicant is eligible to receive an immigrant visa and is admissible for permanent residence (must establish preference eligibility), and
2. The immigrant visa is immediately available at the time the application adjustment is made (the quota is not oversubscribed).

Is this procedure for changing status to a permanent resident without leaving the United States available to all nonimmigrants?

No. This procedure is not available to—

1. alien crewmen;
2. aliens admitted in transit without visas;
3. aliens others than immediate relatives of United States citizens who accepted employment without authorization of the Immigration and Naturalization Service prior to the filing of their application for permanent residence *(Form I-485)*.

Those aliens who cannot change their status in the United States must visit the United States Consul in their native country, obtain immigrant visas from that American Consul, and then be admitted to the United States for lawful permanent residence. However, if the alien is the spouse or unmarried son or daughter of a permanent resident or of a United States citizen, the immigrant visa may be obtained through an American Consulate in Canada.

Legalizing Stay in the United States

Can foreign-born persons become permanent residents if there is no record of their admission to the United States or they are not otherwise eligible for permanent residence?

Yes, they can become permanent residents by a process called "registry."

What are the requirements for "registry"?

Aliens must be able to prove that they—

1. came to the United States before June 30, 1948;
2. resided in the United States ever since;
3. are persons of good moral character;
4. are not barred from the United States under the immigration laws—such as criminals, subversives, smugglers or violators of the narcotics laws.

How does an alien who meets these requirements apply to legalize his or her stay in the United States?

Application is made on *Form I-485, Application for Status as Permanent Resident.* This form, together with *Biographic Information Form G-325A* and *Fingerprint Card FD-258,* two photographs, and a money order or check for $30, is taken or mailed to the nearest office of the Immigration and Naturalization Service.

If applicants prove that they came to the United States before July 1, 1924, what is considered to be their admission date?

If applicants prove that they came to the United States before July 1, 1924, the record of their admission is made as of the date of actual entry into the United States.

If applicants prove that they came to the United States after June 30, 1924, what is considered to be their admission date?

If applicants came to the United States after June 30, 1924, the record of their admission is made as of the date their applications are approved, and they then have to complete the necessary residence and physical presence in the United States for naturalization.

Can aliens who came to the United States illegally on or after June 30, 1948 legalize their stay be creating a record of admission for permanent residence?

It is possible for the Immigration and Naturalization Service to help some of these people. Advice and additional information should be obtained from a social service agency or from a lawyer experienced in handling immigration and naturalization cases.

Naturalization

The 'God and My Country' Flag of thirty-five stars is one of a pair of embroidered silk flags made for the personal use of Civil War General George Brinton McClellan during his political campaign against Lincoln as presidential candidate in 1864.

General Provisions

What is meant by naturalization?

Naturalization is the process by which an alien becomes a citizen of the United States of America.

What is the first step in the naturalization process?

The first step toward naturalization is the submission of a petition for naturalization to the nearest office of the Immigration and Naturalization Service.

How does an alien apply for a petition for naturalization?

Applications are generally made on *Form N-400, Application to File Petition for Naturalization*. This form, and other required forms and instructions, may be obtained free of charge from the nearest office of the Immigration and Naturalization Service, from the clerk of any court which naturalizes aliens, or from any social service agency.

What other forms must be filed with *Form N-400*?

Biographic Information Form G-325A and *Fingerprint Card FD-258* must be filed with *Form N-400*, along with 3 passport-size photographs.

What special precautions must be taken in filling out *Form N-400*?

When completing the form, use a typewriter or print in ink. All items on the form should be answered by applicants to the best of their ability. Be sure to read carefully the instructions attached to the form.

The applicant must spell his or her name exactly as it was spelled upon entry to the United States (as it appears on the *alien registration receipt card*). This is necessary for verifying legal admittance for permanent residence. The alien registration number on the "green card" must also be correctly recorded.

If an alien wishes to have his or her name changed at the time of naturalization, what must be done?

The new name must be placed on Item (4) of the *N-400* form.

May any photographs be submitted with the application for naturalization?

No, the three photographs must be identical, 2 x 2 inches in size, unmounted, printed on thin paper, with a light background. The applicant must be photographed without a hat, showing a full front

view of the features. The photographs must have been taken within
30 days of the date the application is submitted.

Are these photographs submitted unsigned?
Yes, the applicant must submit three unsigned photographs. These
will be signed later by the applicant when he or she appears for
examination.

**Must the *Alien Registration Receipt Card* be sent
with the application?**
No. However, the Alien Registration Number should be written
lightly in pencil on the reverse side of each of the photographs.

**What are the requirements that must be met by
persons applying for naturalization?**
There are basically six requirements for filing a petition for naturalization.

1. *Age:*
   At least 18 years old
2. *Lawful Admission, Residence, and Physical Presence:*
   (a) Must be lawfully admitted to the United States for permanent residence
   (b) Must have resided in the United States as a lawful permanent resident for at least five years*
   (c) Must have been physically present in the United States
   for at least 50 percent of the time necessary to qualify
   (d) For the last six months of the required period of residence, immediately before the filing of the petition,
   must reside in the state where the petition is being filed
3. *Character and Loyalty:*
   (a) Must have good moral character
   (b) Must believe in the principles of the Constitution and
   the form of government of the United States
4. *Allegiance:*
   Must be willing to take an oath of allegiance to the
   United States and renounce all former allegiance
5. *Knowledge of the English Language:*
   Must speak and understand English, as well as read and
   write the language*

* An exception is made for the husband or wife of a United States citizen, who must
be a permanent resident for at least three years.

* However, persons over 50 years of age who have been lawful permanent residents
for at least 20 years may be examined in their native language, be it Spanish, Polish,
German, etc. Also, this requirement does not apply to any person physically unable
to comply, if otherwise qualified to be naturalized.

6. *Knowledge of the United States Government and History:* Must pass an examination to show some understanding of the history and form of government of the United States

Does the continuous residence requirement prevent applicants from being outside the United States during the 5-year period?

No. Applicants may take short visits outside the United States either before or after they apply for naturalization. Under certain circumstances, longer periods of absence over one year are permitted if it can be shown that such persons had not abandoned residence in the United States. However, applicants must have been physically present in the United States for at least half of the required period of residence (2½ years) and in their state of residence for six months.

Does an absence of a year or more within the required period break the required residence?

Yes, unless permission had been obtained from the Immigration and Naturalization Service to be absent for a year or more without breaking the required residence. Request for such permission must generally be made in advance of the absence. Requests that are approved also include the spouse and dependent unmarried sons and daughters who are members of the household and accompany the applicant abroad as dependent members of the household.

Application to obtain such permission must be made on *Form N-470, Application to Preserve Residence for Naturalization Purposes.* A fee of $10 must accompany the application which is filed with the nearest office of the Immigration and Naturalization Service.

Under what conditions may aliens be permitted to be continuously absent from the United States for a year or more and still preserve residence for naturalization purposes?

Permission may be granted for the following reasons:

1. Employment by an American organization
   (a) American firms that are developing foreign trade and commerce for the United States
   (b) American research institutions
   (c) Public international organizations of which the United States is a member
2. Employment by the United States government
3. Service abroad as priests, ministers, missionaries, nuns or sisters by a religious organization based in the United States

Are applicants for naturalization examined on their understanding of American history and American government?

Yes. Applicants are required to demonstrate to the naturalization examiner knowledge and understanding of the fundamentals of the history and of the principles and form of government of the United States.

What is meant by a person of good moral character?

Applicants for naturalization cannot be considered to be of good moral character if, at any time during the five-year period and until they become naturalized, they were or are—

1. habitual drunkards;
2. polygamists, persons connected with prostitution or narcotics, or criminals;
3. adulterers whose activities are deemed to be harmful to the public or to have adverse public effect;
4. convicted gamblers or persons obtaining their principal income from illegal gambling;
5. persons convicted and jailed for 180 days or more;
6. persons who lie under oath for the purpose of gaining benefits under the immigration and naturalization laws.

The disqualifications listed above are not the only reasons for which a person may be found to lack good moral character. Other reasons may be taken into consideration in determining whether an applicant has the good moral character required to become a citizen.

Does membership in the Communist Party or a similar party bar persons from becoming citizens?

Generally, yes. Persons are barred from citizenship if, at any time during the ten-year period just before they file their petition for naturalization in court, they have been members of or affiliated with—

1. the Communist party or a similar party within or outside the United States;
2. any other party or organization that is against all organized government or for world communism, dictatorship in the United States, overthrowing the United States government by force, injuring or killing officers of the United States, or sabotage.

Are there any exceptions to the above provision barring people from becoming citizens?

Yes. If the membership in or affiliation with any of these parties or organizations during the ten-year period was involuntary, or before the age of sixteen, or was a legal requirement for employment, or was used for obtaining food or other necessities of life, persons may become citizens provided they are no longer members of or otherwise affiliated with such parties or organizations.

How are applicants notified to appear for examination?

Applicants are notified by mail by the office of the Immigration and Naturalization Service to which the application forms were sent, when and where to appear for examination.

Are witnesses required for such examination?

No. Witnesses are no longer required.

What happens if the applicant does not meet the naturalization requirements?

If the deficiency is serious, the examiner advises the applicant not to file the petition. If the deficiency can be readily corrected, the examiner might suggest that the petition be filed, but that the examination be postponed until the deficiency is corrected.

If the applicant is found to meet the naturalization requirements, what is the next step?

The applicant files a petition for naturalization. The examiner usually assists the applicant in this step.

Is a fee required for filing such petition?

Yes. The person filing a petition pays a fee of $25 to the clerk of the court. This fee pays for the filing of the petition and also for the naturalization certificate, if and when the certificate is issued.

What happens after the petition for naturalization is filed?

The Immigration and Naturalization Service completes its investigation. After 30 days and after the investigation is completed, the applicant for citizenship is notified to appear in the naturalization court for a final hearing on the petition.

Does the judge question the applicant at the court hearing?

No, the naturalization examiner has already questioned the applicant previously. The judge usually accepts the recommendation of the Immigration and Naturalization Service.

If the Immigration and Naturalization Service recommends that the petition for naturalization be denied, is the applicant informed of such recommendation?

Yes, the applicant is notified of such recommendation before the case is put on the court calendar for final hearing.

May the applicant appeal such recommendation?
Yes. If the applicant feels that the recommendation to deny the petition is unjust, he or she can ask to be examined by the judge in court.

Is the certificate of naturalization issued at the time the petition is granted?
If possible, the certificate is issued at the final hearing. If this cannot be done, the clerk of the court sends the certificate by registered mail at a later date.

Is an oath required when the court grants a petition for naturalization?
Yes. The person whose petition is granted renounces allegiance to the foreign state and promises to support and defend the Constitution and laws of the United States of America.

Are applicants for naturalization required to appear in court?
Yes. However, if the applicant is prevented by sickness or other physical disability from appearing in court, arrangements may be made enabling such applicant to be naturalized without appearing in court.

May a person whose name has been changed or whose naturalization certificate has been lost, mutilated or damaged obtain another copy?
Yes. A duplicate copy of the naturalization certificate may be obtained from the Immigration and Naturalization Service.

How is a duplicate copy of a naturalization certificate obtained?
An application for a duplicate copy must be made on *Form N-565, Application for a New Naturalization or Citizenship Paper.* A check or money order for $10 payable to the Immigration and Naturalization Service must accompany the application.

Do naturalized citizens lose their American citizenship if they join a subversive organization or return to their native country or other foreign country to take up permanent residence?
They may. Any naturalized citizen who within five years following naturalization joins a subversive organization or takes up continuous residence in his or her native country or other foreign country risks loss of American citizenship.

Special Provisions for Certain Groups

Special Provisions for Persons Married to American Citizens

Are there special naturalization provisions for wives and husbands of United States citizens?

Yes. Persons married to American citizens are entitled to special naturalization benefits.

What are these special naturalization benefits?

Persons eligible for these special naturalization benefits may file a petition for naturalization after residing in the United States for only three years if lawfully admitted for permanent residence as a result of the marriage to the United States citizen.

Are all aliens married to American citizens eligible for these special naturalization benefits?

No. These special benefits are only for those persons—

1. who have lived in marital union with the citizen spouses for at least three years;
2. whose spouses have been citizens for the entire three-year period;
3. who have been present physically in the United States for at least half of that period;
4. who have resided in the state in which the petition is being filed for at least six months.

Is special consideration given to applicants whose American spouses are employed abroad?

Yes. The residence and physical presence requirement is waived for applicants whose American spouses are regularly stationed abroad and are—

1. employed by the United States government;
2. employed by an American organization
   (a) American firms that are developing foreign trade and commerce of the United States
   (b) American research institutions
   (c) Public international organizations in which the United States takes part;
3. serving abroad as priests, ministers, or missionaries for a religious organization based in the United States.

However, an applicant must have been lawfully admitted for permanent residence and must prove intention to reside abroad with the citizen spouse and to take up residence in the United States immediately after termination of the spouse's employment abroad.

Other than waiving the residence and physical presence requirement, do husbands and wives of American citizens have other special benefits?

No. They must meet all other requirements for naturalization that generally apply to all aliens.

What proof must the applicant have to obtain a waiver of the residence and physical presence requirement?

The applicant must submit proof of lawful marriage to a citizen of the United States.

How may an applicant prove marriage?

Usually, marriage is proven by submitting a marriage certificate. If either party had been married previously, the termination of such prior marriage must be shown by either a death certificate or a divorce decree.

How may an applicant prove the American citizenship of the spouse?

Proof of American citizenship may be shown by a certificate of birth in the United States, a certificate of citizenship, or a certificate of naturalization.

What happens if the American-born spouse is unable to obtain a birth certificate?

The Immigration and Naturalization Service will advise the applicant how to obtain documentary proof of spouse's citizenship.

Special Provisions for Children of American Citizens

Is a child born abroad to an American citizen, a citizen of the United States by birth?

Unless the parent meets the legal requirements in effect at the time of the child's birth, the child is not an American citizen by birth. These requirements should be checked with the Immigration and Naturalization Service.

Are there special naturalization provisions for such children if they are not United States citizens?

Yes. Children born abroad to American citizens are entitled to special naturalization benefits.

What are these special naturalization benefits?

Children eligible for these special benefits do not have to—

1. speak, read or write English or sign their name;
2. know about the history and form of government of the United States;
3. have lived or been physically present in the United States or in one state for any particular length of time after they have been admitted for permanent residence;
4. take the oath of allegiance if they are too young to understand it.

What are the eligibility requirements for such special naturalization benefits?

An alien child born abroad to an American citizen may be naturalized on a petition filed in the child's behalf by the citizen parent if the child—

1. is under the age of 18 years (naturalization must be completed before the child reaches his 18th birthday);
2. is residing with the parents in the United States;
3. has been lawfully admitted for permanent residence in the United States;
4. takes the oath of citizenship unless excused by the court because the child is too young to understand its meaning.

How is application for such petition made?

Application is made by the citizen parent on *Form N-402, Application to File Petition for Naturalization in Behalf of Child.* This application and three photographs of the child must be filed with the Immigration and Naturalization Service.

Must a biographic information form and a fingerprint card be filed with *Form N-402?*

A biographic information form and a fingerprint card must be filed only if the child is 14 years of age or older.

Does an alien child who has been adopted by an American citizen automatically become a citizen of the United States?

No. The alien child does not become an American citizen by adoption.

Can such an alien child become a naturalized citizen?

Yes, if the naturalization requirements are met.

Are there special naturalization provisions for such a child?

Yes. An alien child adopted by American citizen parents is entitled to special naturalization benefits.

What are these special naturalization benefits?

An adopted alien child eligible for these special benefits does not have to—

1. speak, read, or write English or sign his or her name;
2. know about the history and form of government of the United States;
3. have lived or been physically present in the United States or in a state for any particular length of time after having been lawfully admitted for permanent residence;
4. take the Oath of Allegiance if too young to understand it.

What are the eligibility requirements for such special naturalization benefits?

An alien child adopted by American citizen parents may be naturalized on a petition filed in his or her behalf by the citizen parents if the child—

1. is under the age of 18 years (naturalization must be completed before the child reaches his 18th birthday);
2. was lawfully admitted to the United States for permanent residence;
3. is residing in the United States in the custody of the adoptive parent or parents;
4. takes the Oath of Allegiance unless excused by the court because the child is too young to understand its meaning.

How is application for such petition made?

Application is made by either the adoptive citizen parent or both adoptive parents on *Form N-402, Application to File Petition for Naturalization in Behalf of Child.* This application and three photographs of the child must be filed with the Immigration and Naturalization Service.

Must a biographic information form and a fingerprint card be filed with *Form N-402*?

A biographic information form and a fingerprint card must be filed only if the child is 14 years of age or older.

Special Provisions for Members of the Armed Forces and Veterans

Does an alien become an American citizen merely by serving in the Armed Forces of the United States?

No. Such alien does not automatically become an American citizen by such service.

Are there special naturalization provisions for such an alien?

Yes. An alien who served in the Armed Forces of the United States is entitled to special naturalization benefits.

How is an application for naturalization made under these special provisions?

The necessary forms, as well as additional information, may be obtained from any office of the Immigration and Naturalization Service, from the clerk of any court which naturalizes aliens, or from any veterans' organization.

Is an alien who served with any of the American allies in World War II entitled to special benefits?

No. Such alien is not eligible for such special benefits. These benefits are only for those aliens who served in the Armed Forces of the United States.

Veterans Who Served in Time of War or National Emergency

What are the special naturalization benefits for a veteran who served in time of war or national emergency?

An eligible veteran who served in time of war or national emergency—

1. is not required to prove residence or physical presence within the United States or any one state for any particular time;
2. may file a petition in any naturalization court, regardless of place of residence.

What are the eligibility requirements for such special naturalization benefits?

The requirements for such benefits are as follows:

1. Must have served honorably in an active duty status in the

Armed Forces of the United States at any time during World War I (April 6, 1917 to November 11, 1918), World War II (September 1, 1939 to December 31, 1946), the Korean hostilities (June 25, 1950 to July 1, 1955), the Vietnam hostilities (February 28, 1961 to October 15, 1978), or any other period in which the Armed Forces of the United States were engaged in military operations involving armed conflict with a hostile foreign force

2. Must show lawful admission for permanent residence if he or she was not in the United States, the Panama Canal Zone, American Samoa, or Swains Island at the time of induction, enlistment or re-enlistment

Must a veteran bring witnesses when filing a petition for naturalization?

Witnesses are no longer required when filing a petition for naturalization.

Persons Who Served in Peacetime

Are persons who served in peacetime entitled to the same naturalization benefits given to those who served in time of war or national emergency?

No. They are not entitled to the same naturalization benefits. Different groups who served in peacetime are entitled to different naturalization benefits.

What are these different groups who served in peacetime?

The different groups are:

1. Aliens with continuous service and who apply for naturalization while still in service or within six months after discharge

2. Aliens whose service was not continuous and who apply for naturalization while still in service or within six months after discharge

3. Aliens who apply more than six months after the termination of their service in the Armed Forces of the United States

Group I

Aliens with continuous service and who apply for naturalization while still in service or within six months after discharge

What are the naturalization benefits?

An eligible alien in this group need not comply with all the general naturalization provisions. Such alien—

1. is not required to prove residence in the United States or the state in which the petition is filed, or physical presence in the United States for any particular time;
2. may file a petition in any naturalization court, regardless of place of residence.

What are the eligibility requirements?

The requirements for such benefits are as follows:

1. Honorable service in the Armed Forces of the United States for a continuous period of three years
2. Application for naturalization is made while still in service or not later than six months after discharge from the service

Group II

Aliens whose service was not continuous and who apply for naturalization while still in service or within six months after discharge

What are the naturalization benefits?

Eligible aliens in this group must prove residence in the United States and the state in which the petition is filed, good moral character, and belief in the principles of the Constitution of the United States. They must also prove that they are favorable toward the good order and happiness of the United States. For the five years immediately preceding the date of filing such petition while they were out of service, they must prove residence and other qualifications for naturalization; however, they may file their petition in any naturalization court regardless of place of residence.

What are the eligibility requirements?

The requirements for such benefits are—

1. honorable service in the armed forces of the United States for periods totaling three years, and
2. application for naturalization made while in the service or not later than six months after discharge from the service.

Group III

Aliens who apply more than six months after ending their service in the Armed Forces of the United States

What are the naturalization benefits?
An eligible alien in this group must comply with all the general naturalization provisions. However, service during the five years immediately preceding the date of filing the petition is considered as residence and physical presence in the United States.

What is the eligibility requirement for such special naturalization benefits?
The requirement for such benefits is proof of honorable service in the Armed Forces of the United States for three years.

Special Provisions for Seamen

Are there special naturalization provisions for seamen?
Yes. Seamen who meet certain conditions receive special naturalization benefits.

What are these special naturalization benefits?
Seamen eligible for these benefits are exempted in part from the general residence and physical presence requirement for naturalization. Time served at sea outside the United States can be counted as residence and physical presence in the United States.

What are the eligibility requirements for such special naturalization privileges?
The eligibility requirements are:

1. Service as a seaman must have been performed on board a vessel—
   a. operated by the United States or by an agency owned by the United States;
   b. with its home port in the United States and registered under the laws of the United States; or
   c. with its home port in the United States and owned by an American citizen or by an American corporation; and
2. Service performed was—
   a. honorable or with good conduct;
   b. after lawful admission to the United States for permanent residence; and
   c. within five years of the date of filing petition for naturalization.

Special Provisions for Former Citizens

Are there special naturalization provisions for former citizens who wish to regain citizenship?

Yes. Several groups of former citizens are entitled to special naturalization benefits.

What are the different groups of former citizens who are entitled to special naturalization benefits?

The different groups are:

1. Women who lost citizenship by marriage to aliens
2. Persons who lost citizenship by serving in the armed forces of certain foreign countries during World War II

Group I

Women Who Lost Citizenship by Marriage to Aliens

When did women lose their citizenship by marriage to aliens?

A female American citizen who married an alien before September 22, 1922, or who married an alien ineligible for citizenship between September 22, 1922, and March 3, 1931, lost her American citizenship if she entered into the marriage with the intention of giving up her American citizenship.

What are the naturalization benefits for women in this group who lost citizenship by marriage to aliens?

A woman in this group must comply with all general naturalization provisions, with the following exceptions:

1. She is not required to prove residence or physical presence in the United States or the state in which the petition is filed.
2. Her petition need not set forth that it is her intention to reside permanently in the United States.
3. She may file her petition in any naturalization court regardless of place of residence.

Group II

Persons Who Lost Citizenship by Serving in the Armed Forces of Certain Foreign Countries during World War II

Are all veterans of the armed forces of American allies entitled to special naturalization benefits?

No, they are not eligible for any special benefits. These special benefits are only for persons who were American citizens just prior to joining the armed forces of countries not at war with the United States during World War II.

What are the special naturalization benefits for such persons who lost their American citizenship?

Persons eligible for such special benefits—

1. may file their petitions in any naturalization court regardless of place of residence;
2. are not required to prove residence or physical presence in the United States or state in which the petition is filed after admission for permanent residence.

What are the eligibility requirements for such benefits?

The requirements for eligibility are as follows:

1. Service in the armed forces of the foreign country must have occurred between September 1, 1939, and September 2, 1945.
2. Such foreign country was not at war with the United States during any period of service.
3. Such foreign country fought against a country with which the United States was at war after December 7, 1941, and before September 2, 1945.

Other Documents

Declaration of Intention

Must a person file a declaration of intention in order to become an American citizen?

No. At one time, a declaration of intention or "first paper" was a requirement for naturalization. Since 1952, this has no longer been a requirement.

Can a declaration of intention still be filed?

Yes. A declaration of intention may be filed if it is needed in order to obtain a job or a license.

What are the requirements for filing a declaration of intention?

The only requirements are that the applicant be at least 18 years old and lawfully admitted to the United States for permanent residence.

Is such applicant required to be able to read, write and speak English, and pass an examination on the history and form of government of the United States?

No. There are no educational requirements for obtaining a declaration of intention. In fact, the applicant may sign the declaration of intention in any language or by making a mark.

How is application for a declaration of intention made?

Form N-300, Application to File Declaration of Intention, and instructions may be obtained without cost from any office of the Immigration and Naturalization Service, from the clerk of a naturalization court, or from most social service agencies. The completed application and three photographs must be taken or mailed to the nearest office of the Immigration and Naturalization Service. A $5 fee must be paid when the copy of the declaration of intention is obtained from the court clerk.

Certificate of Citizenship

What is a Certificate of Citizenship?

Form N-562, Certificate of Citizenship, is issued by the Immigration and Naturalization Service to a wife or child who became an American citizen automatically through a husband or parent.

What is meant by becoming a citizen automatically through a husband or parent?

An alien woman who married an American citizen before September 22, 1922, may automatically become an American citizen as a result of such marriage. A child born in a foreign country of an American citizen parent or parents may have become an American citizen at birth. American citizenship may be acquired automatically in many other instances.

How is a Certificate of Citizenship obtained?

Application is made on Form N-600, Application for Certificate of Citizenship. This form, together with three photographs and a money order or check for $15.00 is taken or mailed to the nearest office of the Immigration and Naturalization Service.

Are official documents required to be submitted with the application?

Required documents regarding birth, marriage, death, divorce, etc., must be submitted with the application. Any document in a foreign language must be accompanied by a certified English translation.

What if the applicant is unable to obtain any of the required documents?

The applicant must explain why he or she is unable to furnish the required documents and must forward for consideration secondary evidence. Baptismal certificates, school records or census records may be submitted to verify date and place of birth. Notarized affidavits of persons, who were living at the time and who have personal knowledge of the event, may be submitted to verify date and place of birth, marriage, death, divorce, etc.

Would failure to apply for a Certificate of Citizenship jeopardize a person's citizenship?

No. Failure to apply for such a certificate would not in any way affect a person's citizenship, but it is one way of showing official recognition of citizenship. Another way is by applying for a U.S. passport.

Replacement of Documents

Can a person whose declaration of intention, certificate of citizenship or certificate of naturalization has been lost, damaged or destroyed obtain a new declaration or certificate?

Yes, he or she can apply for a new declaration or certificate.

How does a person obtain a new declaration or certificate?

Application is made on *Form N-565, Application for a New Naturalization or Citizenship Paper.* This completed form, two photographs and a money order or check for $10 are taken or mailed to the nearest office of the Immigration and Naturalization Service.

Can a person whose name has been changed by a court or by marriage after naturalization obtain a new declaration of intention, certificate of citizenship or certificate of naturalization?

Yes, such person can apply for a new declaration or certificate by using *Form N-565* and the same procedure as outlined above. In addition, proof of changed name must be submitted by attaching a marriage certificate or court document.

Loss of American Citizenship

Can American citizenship be taken away?

Although every United States citizen, whether by birth or naturalization, has a constitutional right to remain a citizen, certain acts indicating that the person voluntarily relinquished that citizenship can result in loss of American citizenship.

Is this a major problem for citizens living in the United States?

Generally, no. However, citizens who plan to live abroad and who wish to retain their American citizenship should know how such citizenship may be lost.

What acts may result in loss of American citizenship?

Examples of acts which indicate intention to relinquish American citizenship and which may result in loss of such citizenship are:

1. Being naturalized in a foreign state
2. Taking a formal oath of allegiance to a foreign state
3. Serving in the armed forces of a foreign state engaged in hostilities against the United States
4. Serving in an important political post in a foreign government
5. Renouncing American citizenship before an American diplomatic or consular officer abroad
6. Making a formal renunciation of American citizenship in time of war before an officer designated by the attorney general of the United States
7. Committing and being convicted of any act of treason against the United States, or attempting by force to overthrow it, or bearing arms or conspiring against it

The above acts must be done with the specific intention of abandoning United States citizenship.

Commonly Used Immigration and Naturalization Forms

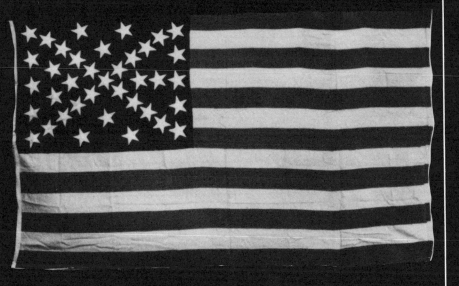

The Hour-Glass Flag of thirty-eight stars is a flag of the First Centennial era. Circa 1876-77.

176

NAME (Last in CAPS)   (First)   (Middle)

I AM IN THE UNITED STATES AS:
- ☐ Visitor   ☐ Permanent Resident
- ☐ Student   ☐ Other_____
  (Specify)

COUNTRY OF CITIZENSHIP | DATE OF BIRTH

COPY NUMBER FROM ALIEN CARD

A

PRESENT ADDRESS   (Street or rural route)   (City or Post Office)   (State)   (ZIP Code)

(IF ABOVE ADDRESS IS TEMPORARY) I expect to remain there _____ years _____ months

LAST ADDRESS   (Street or rural route)   (City or Post Office)   (State)   (ZIP Code)

I WORK FOR OR ATTEND SCHOOL AT: (Employer's Name or Name of School)

(Street Addresss or rural route)   (City or Post Office)   (State)   (ZIP Code)

PORT OF ENTRY INTO U.S. | DATE OF ENTRY INTO U.S. | IF NOT A PERMANENT RESIDENT, MY STAY IN THE U.S. EXPIRES ON: (Date)

SIGNATURE | DATE

AR-11 (Rev. 9-27-75)N   GPO 957-809   OMB Appvd. No. 43-R0038

ALIEN'S CHANGE OF ADDRESS CARD

(THIS CARD IS NOT TO BE USED FOR THE ANNUAL REPORT REQUIRED UNDER THE IMMIGRATION AND NATIONALITY ACT BETWEEN JANUARY 1 AND JANUARY 31 OF EACH YEAR. IT IS TO BE USED BY ALL ALIENS TO REPORT CHANGE OF ADDRESS WITHIN 10 DAYS OF SUCH CHANGE, AND BY VISITORS AND OTHER ALIENS IN TEMPORARY STATUS TO REPORT THEIR PLACE OF RESIDENCE EACH 3 MONTHS.)

REQUIRED BY SEC. 265 I&N ACT (8 USC 1305) DATA USED BY INS FOR STATISTICAL &RECORDS PURPOSES & MAY BE FURNISHED FEDERAL,STATE,LOCAL & FOREIGN LAW ENFORCEMENT OFFICIALS. INEXCUSABLE FAILURE TO REPORT PUNISHABLE BY FINE OR IMPRISONMENT AND/OR DEPORTATION

This card is not evidence of identity, age, or status claimed

PLACE STAMP HERE

DEPARTMENT OF JUSTICE
Immigration and Naturalization Service
Washington, D.C. 20536

AR-11   Alien's Change of Address Card

OMB Approval No. 44-R1301

U.S. DEPARTMENT OF LABOR
Employment and Training Administration

APPLICATION
FOR
ALIEN EMPLOYMENT CERTIFICATION

IMPORTANT: READ CAREFULLY BEFORE COMPLETING THIS FORM

PRINT legibly in ink or use a typewriter. If you need more space to answer questions on this form, use a separate sheet. Identify each answer with the number of the corresponding question. SIGN AND DATE each sheet in original signature.

To knowingly furnish any false information in the preparation of this form and any supplement thereto or to aid, abet, or counsel another to do so is a felony punishable by $10,000 fine or 5 years in the penitentiary, or both (18 U.S.C. 1001).

PART A. OFFER OF EMPLOYMENT

1. Name of Alien   (Family name in capital letter, First, Middle, Maiden)

2. Present Address of Alien   (Number, Street, City and Town, State ZIP Code or Province, Country)

3. Type of Visa   (If in U.S.)

The following information is submitted as evidence of an offer of employment.

4. Name of Employer   (Full name of organization)

5. Telephone   (Area Code and Number)

6. Address   (Number, Street, City or Town, Country, State, ZIP Code)

7. Address Where Alien Will Work   (if different from item 6)

8. Nature of Employer's Business Activity	9. Name of Job Title	10. Total Hours Per Week		11. Work Schedule (Hourly)	12. Rate of Pay	
		a. Basic	b. Overtime		a. Basic	b. Overtime
				a.m. p.m.	$ per	$ per hour

13. Describe Fully the Job to be Performed   (Duties)

14. State in detail the MINIMUM education, training, and experience for a worker to perform satisfactorily the job duties described in item 13 above.

15. Other Special Requirements

EDU- CATION (Enter number of years)	Grade School	High School	College	College Degree Required (specify)
				Major Field of Study

TRAIN- ING	No. Yrs.	No. Mos.	Type of Training

EXPERI- ENCE	Job Offered		Related Occupation	Related Occupation (specify)
	Number			
	Yrs.	Mos.	Yrs.	Mos.

16. Occupational Title of Person Who Will Be Alien's Immediate Supervisor

17. Number of Employees Alien will Supervise

ENDORSEMENTS   (Make no entry in section - for government use only)

Date Forms Received

L.O.	S.O.
R.O.	N.O.
Ind. Code	Occ. Code
Occ. Title	

Replaces MA 7-50A, B and C (Apr. 1970 edition) which is obsolete.

ETA 750 (Oct. 1979)

ETA-750   Application for Alien Employment Certification

178

<table>
<tr><td colspan="2">18. COMPLETE ITEMS ONLY IF JOB IS TEMPORARY</td><td colspan="2">19. IF JOB IS UNIONIZED   (Complete)</td></tr>
<tr><td>a. No. of Openings To Be Filled By Aliens Under Job Offer</td><td>b. Exact Dates You Expect To Employ Alien
From   To</td><td>a. Number of Local</td><td>b. Name of Local</td></tr>
<tr><td></td><td></td><td></td><td>c. City and State</td></tr>
</table>

20. STATEMENT FOR LIVE-AT-WORK JOB OFFERS   *(Complete for Private Household Job ONLY)*

<table>
<tr><td colspan="2">a. Description of Residence</td><td colspan="4">b. No. Persons Residing at Place of Employment</td><td rowspan="2">c. Will free board and private room not shared with anyone be provided?</td><td rowspan="2">("X" one)
☐ YES ☐ NO</td></tr>
<tr><td>("X" one)
☐ House
☐ Apartment</td><td>Number of Rooms</td><td>Adults</td><td>BOYS
GIRLS</td><td>Children</td><td>Ages</td></tr>
</table>

21. DESCRIBE EFFORTS TO RECRUIT U.S. WORKERS AND THE RESULTS. *(Specify Sources of Recruitment by Name)*

22. Applications require various types of documentation. Please read PART II of the instructions to assure that appropriate supporting documentation is included with your application.

23. EMPLOYER CERTIFICATIONS

By virtue of my signature below, I HEREBY CERTIFY the following conditions of employment.

a. I have enough funds available to pay the wage or salary offered the alien.

b. The wage offered equals or exceeds the prevailing wage and I guarantee that, if a labor certification is granted, the wage paid to the alien when the alien begins work will equal or exceed the prevailing wage which is applicable at the time the alien begins work.

c. The wage offered is not based on commissions, bonuses, or other incentives, unless I guarantee a wage paid on a weekly, bi-weekly or monthly basis.

d. I will be able to place the alien on the payroll on or before the date of the alien's proposed entrance into the United States.

e. The job opportunity does not involve unlawful discrimination by race, creed, color, national origin, age, sex, religion, handicap, or citizenship.

f. The job opportunity is not:

   (1) Vacant because the former occupant is on strike or is being locked out in the course of a labor dispute involving a work stoppage.

   (2) At issue in a labor dispute involving a work stoppage.

g. The job opportunity's terms, conditions and occupational environment are not contrary to Federal, State or local law.

h. The job opportunity has been and is clearly open to any qualified U.S. worker.

24. DECLARATIONS

DECLARATION OF EMPLOYER ▶ Pursuant to 28 U.S.C. 1746, I declare under penalty of perjury the foregoing is true and correct.

SIGNATURE		DATE
NAME (Type or Print)	TITLE	

AUTHORIZATION OF AGENT OF EMPLOYER ▶ I HEREBY DESIGNATE the agent below to represent me for the purposes of labor certification and I TAKE FULL RESPONSIBILITY for accuracy of any representations made by my agent.

SIGNATURE OF EMPLOYER		DATE
NAME OF AGENT (Type or Print)	ADDRESS OF AGENT (Number, Street, City, State, ZIP Code)	

ETA-750   Page 2

PART B. STATEMENT OF QUALIFICATIONS OF ALIEN

FOR ADVICE CONCERNING REQUIREMENTS FOR ALIEN EMPLOYMENT CERTIFICATION: *If alien is in the U.S., contact nearest office of Immigration and Naturalization Service. If alien is outside U.S., contact nearest U.S. Consulate.*
IMPORTANT: READ ATTACHED INSTRUCTIONS BEFORE COMPLETING THIS FORM.
Print legibly in ink or use a typewriter. If you need more space to fully answer any questions on this form, use a separate sheet. Identify each answer with the number of the corresponding question. Sign and date each sheet.

1. Name of Alien *(Family name in capital letters)* | First name | Middle name | Maiden name

2. Present Address *(No., Street, City or Town, State or Province and ZIP Code* | Country | 3. Type of Visa *(If in U.S.)*

4. Alien's Birthdate *(Month, Day, Year)* | 5. Birthplace *(City or Town, State or Province)* | Country | 6. Present Nationality or Citizenship *(Country)*

7. Address in United States Where Alien Will Reside

8. Name and Address of Prospective Employer if Alien has job offer in U.S. | 9. Occupation in which Alien is Seeking Work

10. "X" the appropriate box below and furnish the information required for the box marked
a. ☐ Alien will apply for a visa abroad at the American Consulate in — | City in Foreign Country | Foreign Country
b. ☐ Alien is in the United States and will apply for adjustment of status to that of a lawful permanent resident in the office of the Immigration and Naturalization Service at — | City | State

11. Names and Addresses of Schools, Colleges and Universities Attended *(Include trade or vocational training facilities)* | Field of Study | FROM Month/Year | TO Month/Year | Degrees or Certificates Received

SPECIAL QUALIFICATIONS AND SKILLS

12. Additional Qualifications and Skills Alien Possesses and Proficiency in the use of Tools, Machines or Equipment Which Would Help Establish if Alien Meets Requirements for Occupation in Item 9.

13. List Licenses *(Professional, journeyman, etc.)*

14. List Documents Attached Which are Submitted as Evidence that Alien Possesses the Education, Training, Experience, and Abilities Represented

Endorsements | DATE REC. DOL | O.T. & C.

(Make no entry in this section — FOR Government Agency USE ONLY)

(Items continued on next page)

ETA-750 Page 3

15. WORK EXPERIENCE. *List all jobs held during past three (3) years. Also, list any other jobs related to the occupation for which the alien is seeking certification as indicated in item 9.*

a. NAME AND ADDRESS OF EMPLOYER

NAME OF JOB	DATE STARTED Month	Year	DATE LEFT Month	Year	KIND OF BUSINESS

DESCRIBE IN DETAILS THE DUTIES PERFORMED, INCLUDING THE USE OF TOOLS, MACHINES, OR EQUIPMENT	NO. OF HOURS PER WEEK

b. NAME AND ADDRESS OF EMPLOYER

NAME OF JOB	DATE STARTED Month	Year	DATE LEFT Month	Year	KIND OF BUSINESS

DESCRIBE IN DETAIL THE DUTIES PERFORMED, INCLUDING THE USE OF TOOLS, MACHINES, OR EQUIPMENT	NO. OF HOURS PER WEEK

c. NAME AND ADDRESS OF EMPLOYER

NAME OF JOB	DATE STARTED Month	Year	DATE LEFT Month	Year	KIND OF BUSINESS

DESCRIBE IN DETAIL THE DUTIES PERFORMED, INCLUDING THE USE OF TOOLS, MACHINES, OR EQUIPMENT	NO. OF HOURS PER WEEK

16. DECLARATIONS

DECLARATION OF ALIEN ► ► *Pursuant to 28 U.S.C. 1746, I declare under penalty of perjury the foregoing is true and correct.*

SIGNATURE OF ALIEN	DATE

AUTHORIZATION OF AGENT OF ALIEN ► ► *I hereby designate the agent below to represent me for the purposes of labor certification and I take full responsibility for accuracy of any representations made by my agent.*

SIGNATURE OF ALIEN	DATE

NAME OF AGENT (Type or print)	ADDRESS OF AGENT (No., Street, City, State, ZIP Code)

ETA-750   Page 4

APPLICANT	LEAVE BLANK	TYPE OR PRINT ALL INFORMATION IN BLACK	FBI LEAVE BLANK

LAST NAME **NAM**   FIRST NAME   MIDDLE NAME

SIGNATURE OF PERSON FINGERPRINTED

ALIASES **AKA**   ORI

RESIDENCE OF PERSON FINGERPRINTED

DATE OF BIRTH **DOB** Month Day Year

CITIZENSHIP **CTZ**   SEX RACE HGT WGT EYES HAIR PLACE OF BIRTH **POB**

DATE   SIGNATURE OF OFFICIAL TAKING FINGERPRINTS

YOUR NO. **OCA**   LEAVE BLANK

EMPLOYER AND ADDRESS

FBI NO. **FBI**   CLASS

ARMED FORCES NO. **MNU**   REF.

REASON FINGERPRINTED

SOCIAL SECURITY NO. **SOC**

MISCELLANEOUS NO. **MNU**

1. R. THUMB   2. R. INDEX   3. R. MIDDLE   4. R. RING   5. R. LITTLE

6. L. THUMB   7. L. INDEX   8. L. MIDDLE   9. L. RING   10. L. LITTLE

LEFT FOUR FINGERS TAKEN SIMULTANEOUSLY   L. THUMB   R. THUMB   RIGHT FOUR FINGERS TAKEN SIMULTANEOUSLY

FD-258   Fingerprint Card

182

FORM G-325 (REV. 6-1-74) Y
BIOGRAPHIC
INFORMATION

UNITED STATES DEPARTMENT OF JUSTICE
Immigration and Naturalization Service

Form Approved
OMB No. 43-R436

(Family name)	(First name)		(Middle name)	☐ MALE ☐ FEMALE	BIRTHDATE (Mo.-Day-Yr.)	NATIONALITY	ALIEN REGISTRATION NO. (If any)
ALL OTHER NAMES USED (Including names by previous marriages)				CITY AND COUNTRY OF BIRTH			SOCIAL SECURITY NO. (If any)

	FAMILY NAME	FIRST NAME	DATE, CITY AND COUNTRY OF BIRTH (If known)	CITY AND COUNTRY OF RESIDENCE
FATHER				
MOTHER (Maiden name)				

HUSBAND (If none, so state) OR WIFE	FAMILY NAME (For wife, give maiden name)	FIRST NAME	BIRTHDATE	CITY & COUNTRY OF BIRTH	DATE OF MARRIAGE	PLACE OF MARRIAGE
FORMER HUSBANDS OR WIVES (If none, so state)						

FAMILY NAME (For wife, give maiden name)	FIRST NAME	BIRTHDATE	DATE AND PLACE OF MARRIAGE	DATE AND PLACE OF TERMINATION OF MARRIAGE

APPLICANT'S RESIDENCE LAST FIVE YEARS. LIST PRESENT ADDRESS FIRST.

STREET AND NUMBER	CITY	PROVINCE OR STATE	COUNTRY	FROM MONTH	FROM YEAR	TO MONTH	TO YEAR
						PRESENT TIME	

APPLICANT'S LAST ADDRESS OUTSIDE THE UNITED STATES OF MORE THAN ONE YEAR.

STREET AND NUMBER	CITY	PROVINCE OR STATE	COUNTRY	FROM MONTH	FROM YEAR	TO MONTH	TO YEAR

APPLICANT'S EMPLOYMENT LAST FIVE YEARS. (IF NONE, SO STATE.) LIST PRESENT EMPLOYMENT FIRST.

FULL NAME AND ADDRESS OF EMPLOYER	OCCUPATION (Specify)	FROM MONTH	FROM YEAR	TO MONTH	TO YEAR
				PRESENT TIME	

Show below last occupation abroad if not shown above. (Include all information requested above.)

THIS FORM IS SUBMITTED IN CONNECTION WITH APPLICATION FOR:
☐ NATURALIZATION ☐ OTHER (SPECIFY)
☐ ADJUSTMENT OF STATUS

SIGNATURE OF APPLICANT OR PETITIONER   DATE

Are all copies legible? ☐ Yes

IF YOUR NATIVE ALPHABET IS IN OTHER THAN ROMAN LETTERS, WRITE YOUR NAME IN YOUR NATIVE ALPHABET IN THIS SPACE

PENALTIES: SEVERE PENALTIES ARE PROVIDED BY LAW FOR KNOWINGLY AND WILLFULLY FALSIFYING OR CONCEALING A MATERIAL FACT.

APPLICANT:
BE SURE TO PUT YOUR NAME AND ALIEN REGISTRATION NUMBER IN THE BOX OUTLINED BY HEAVY BORDER BELOW.

COMPLETE THIS BOX (Family name)	(Given name)	(Middle name)	(Alien registration number)

(OTHER AGENCY USE)

INS USE (Office of Origin)
OFFICE CODE:
TYPE OF CASE:
DATE:

FORM G-325 A   [1] Ident.

G-325   Biographic Information

ALIEN ADDRESS REPORT COMPLETE ALL ITEMS—PRINT IN BLOCK LETTERS WITH BALL-POINT PEN OR USE TYPEWRITER. THIS CARD MUST BE MAILED. PLACE A TEN CENT U.S. POSTAGE STAMP ON REVERSE AND DROP IN MAIL BOX. THIS CARD IS REVISED ANNUALLY. ONLY SUBMIT A CURRENT YEAR CARD.

1. (LAST NAME)   (FIRST)   (MIDDLE)

2. ADDRESS IN THE U.S. (EXCEPT COMMUTERS—SHOW ADDRESS IN MEXICO OR CANADA. SEE ITEM 15)

| CITY OR TOWN | STATE | ZIP CODE | CHECK HERE IF ADDRESS IS CURRENT ☐ |

3. ALIEN NO. FROM ALIEN CARD A-   4. PLACE ENTERED THE U.S.   5. WHEN ENTERED U.S. (MO/DAY/YR)   6. SEX ☐ MALE ☐ FEMALE

7. COUNTRY OF BIRTH   8. DATE OF BIRTH (MO/DAY/YR)   9. COUNTRY OF CITIZENSHIP   10. ARE YOU NOW WORKING IN THE U.S.? ☐ YES ☐ NO

11. SOCIAL SECURITY NO. (IF ANY)   12. FOR GOVERNMENT USE ONLY

13. PRESENT OR MOST RECENT OCCUPATION IN U.S. (MAIN JOB)   14. TYPE OF FIRM OR BUSINESS OF PRESENT OR MOST RECENT EMPLOYMENT (MAIN JOB)

15. STATUS (CHECK APPROPRIATE BOX) WHEN DID YOU RECEIVE YOUR PRESENT IMMIGRATION STATUS? (MO/DAY/YR)_____

1 ☐ IMMIGRANT (PERMANENT RESIDENT)   3 ☐ VISITOR   4 ☐ CPEWMAN   5 ☐ STUDENT
2 ☐ IMMIGRANT (COMMUTER WORKER-CHECK THIS BLOCK   6 ☐ EXCHANGE ALIEN   7 ☐ REFUGEE-PAROLEE
IF YOU ENTER THE U.S. DAILY OR AT LEAST TWICE A WEEK)   8 ☐ OTHER (SPECIFY)_____

16. I CERTIFY THAT THE STATEMENTS ON THIS CARD ARE TRUE TO THE BEST OF MY KNOWLEDGE

SIGNATURE (IF UNDER 14 YEARS OLD, SIGNATURE OF PARENT OR GUARDIAN)   DATE

Form I-53 (Rev 1 1 81Y)   U.S. DEPARTMENT OF JUSTICE—IMMIGRATION AND NATURALIZATION SERVICE   FORM APPROVED OMB NO. 43-R0306

I-53   Alien Address Report

U. S. DEPARTMENT OF JUSTICE
Immigration and Naturalization Service

Form Approved
OMB No. 43-R0040

(SEE INSTRUCTIONS ON REVERSE)

Fee Stamp

APPLICATION BY A LAWFUL PERMANENT RESIDENT FOR
AN ALIEN REGISTRATION RECEIPT CARD, FORM I-551
(TYPE OR PRINT IN BLOCK LETTERS WITH BALLPOINT PEN)

1. Family Name (Capital Letters)	First	Middle	2. Alien Registration Number A-

3. Mailing address in U. S.	c/o	(Number & Street)	(City)	(State)	(ZIP Code)

4. Name used when I became a permanent resident: (If same as present, write "Same")

5. Country of citizenship

6. Date of Birth (Mo./Day/Yr.)

7. Place of birth (City or town)(Province or State) (Country)

8. My phone number is (Include Area Code)

9. Originally admitted to U.S. at (City and State)

10. Date of admission as Permanent Resident or adjusted to status as Permanent Resident (Mo./Day/Yr)

11. Destination in U.S. at time of original admission

12. My file is at the INS office in (City and State)

13. List the dates of all absences from the U. S. of 1 year or longer, since admission for permanent residence

14. City of residence when I applied for an immigrant visa or adjustment to permanent residence status

15. Consulate where my visa was issued (or INS office where I was adjusted to permanent residence status)

16. Mother's First Name ☐ Living ☐ Deceased

17. Father's First Name ☐ Living ☐ Deceased

18. I NEED A CARD BECAUSE:

(A) ☐ My alien registration receipt card was lost, destroyed, or mutilated. (Attach remainder of card) (FEE REQUIRED, SEE INSTRUCTION 3.) Explain how card was lost, destroyed, or mutilated.

(B) ☐ My name has been changed. (Attach the decree of the court or the marriage certificate and old card.) (FEE REQUIRED, SEE INSTRUCTION 3)

(C) ☐ I am required to be registered and fingerprinted after my 14th birthday. (Attach old Card.) (You MUST use the fingerprint card Form FD-258 which you can get from any United States Consular or Immigration and Naturalization Service office.)

(D) ☐ I am an alien commuter taking up actual permanent residence in the U. S. (Attach old card.)

(E) ☐ I received an incorrect card. (Attach old card.)

(F) ☐ I never received my card.

(G) ☐ OTHER (Explain)

19. Signature and date of person preparing the form if other than applicant

20. Signature of applicant and date

DO NOT WRITE BELOW THIS LINE.
ACTION BLOCK (For use by Immigration or Consular officer) This applicant was interviewed by me under oath on _____

at _____ (City)   (Date)

REMARKS:

(Signature and Title)

☐ GRANTED   ☐ DENIED

DATE OF ACTION
DD
DISTRICT

(Signature of Immigration Officer)

☐ Fingerprint card forwarded to the FBI to comply with Section 262 b _____ (Initials and Date)

☐ I-89 to Immigration Card Facility _____ (Date)

FORM I-90 (Rev. 4-4-80) N

RECEIVED	TRANS. IN	RET'D. TRANS. OUT	COMPLETED

I-90   Application by a Lawful Permanent Resident for an Alien Registration Card, Form I-551

UNITED STATES DEPARTMENT OF JUSTICE

Immigration and Naturalization Service

Form Approved

OMB NO. 43—RO 401

Fee Stamp

PETITION TO CLASSIFY STATUS OF ALIEN RELATIVE FOR ISSUANCE OF IMMIGRANT VISA

PLEASE NOTE YOU ARE THE PETITIONER AND YOUR RELATIVE IS THE BENEFICIARY

1. Name of beneficiary (Last, in CAPS) (First) (Middle)

2. Do Not Write in This Space

3. Names, birthdates and countries of birth of beneficiary's children:

4. Other names used: (including maiden name if married)

5. Country of beneficiary's birth

6. Date of beneficiary's birth (Month, day, year)

7. My name is: (Last, in CAPS) (First) (Middle)

8. My phone number is:

9. Other names used: (including maiden name if married woman)

10. Relationship of beneficiary to myself

11. I was born: (Month) (Day) (Year) in: (Town or city) (State or Province) (Country)

12. If you are a citizen of the United States, give the following:
a. Citizenship was acquired: (Check one)

☐ through birth in the U.S. ☐ through parents ☐ through naturalization ☐ through marriage

(1) If acquired through naturalization, give name under which naturalized, number of naturalization certificate, and date and place of naturalization:

(2) If known, my former alien registration was A _____

(3) If acquired through parentage or marriage, have you obtained a certificate of citizenship in your own name?_____

(a) If so, give number of certificate and date and place of issuance: _____

(b) If not, submit evidence of citizenship in accordance with instruction 3 a (2)

13. If you are a lawful permanent resident alien of the United States, give the following:
a. Alien Registration Number:
A—

b. Date, place, and means of admission for lawful permanent residence

14. Beneficiary's marital status:
☐ Married ☐ Widowed ☐ Divorced ☐ Single

15. Name of beneficiary's spouse, if married, and date and country of birth (Omit this item if petition is for your spouse)

16. Full address of beneficiary's spouse and children, if any (Omit this item if petition is for your spouse)

17. If this petition is for your spouse or child, give the following:
a. Date and place of your present marriage

b. Names of my prior spouses

c. Names of spouse's prior spouses

18. Has this beneficiary ever been in the U.S.?
☐ YES ☐ NO

19. Are beneficiary and petitioner related by adoption?
☐ YES ☐ NO

—(CONTINUE WITH ITEM 20 ON REVERSE)—

OATH OR AFFIRMATION OF PETITIONER

I swear (affirm) that I know the contents of this petition signed by me and that the statements herein are true and correct.

Signature of petitioner (See Instruction No. 5) . . . .

Subscribed and sworn to (affirmed) before me this _____ day of _____ 19_____ at _____

(SEAL) My commission expires _____ (SIGNATURE OF OFFICER ADMINISTERING OATH) (TITLE)

SIGNATURE OF PERSON PREPARING FORM IF OTHER THAN PETITIONER

I declare that this document was prepared by me at the request of the petitioner and is based on all information of which I have any knowledge.

(SIGNATURE) (ADDRESS) (DATE)

RECEIVED	TRANS. IN	RET'D. TRANS. OUT	COMPLETED

FORM I—130 (Rev. 10-26-79) N

I-130   Petition to Classify Status of Alien Relative for Issuance of Immigrant Visa

186

TO THE SECRETARY OF STATE:

The petition was filed on ---

The petition is approved for status under section:

☐ 201 *(b)* CHILD SPOUSE.

☐ 201 *(b)* PARENT

☐ 203 *(a)* **(1)**

☐ 203 *(a)* **(2)**

☐ 203 *(a)* **(4)**

☐ 203 *(a)* **(5)**

DATE OF ACTION

DD

DISTRICT

REMARKS

☐ PERSONAL INTERVIEW CONDUCTED
☐ DOCUMENT CHECK ONLY
☐ FIELD INVESTIGATION COMPLETED
☐ APPROVAL PREVIOUSLY FORWARDED

REMARKS (Continued)

(PETITIONER IS NOT TO WRITE ABOVE THIS LINE)

20. Check the appropriate box below and furnish the information required for the box checked:

☐ Beneficiary will apply for a visa abroad at the American Consulate in _____
   (CITY IN FOREIGN COUNTRY) (FOREIGN COUNTRY)

☐ Beneficiary is in the United States and will apply for adjustment of status to that of a lawful permanent resident in the office of the Immigration and Naturalization Service at_____
   (CITY)   (STATE)

If the application for adjustment of status is denied, the beneficiary will apply for a visa abroad at the American Consulate in _____
(CITY IN FOREIGN COUNTRY)   (FOREIGN COUNTRY)

21. My residence in the United States is: (C/O, if appropriate)   (Apt. No.)   (Number and Street)   (Town or city)   (State)   (ZIP Code)

22. My address abroad (if any) is: (Number and street)   (Town or city)   (Province)   (Country)

23. Last address at which I and my spouse resided together
   (Town or city)   (State or Province)   (Country)   (Apt. No.)   (Number and street)   From (Month) (Year)   To (Month) (Year)

24. Address in the United States where beneficiary will reside   (City)   (State)

25. Address at which beneficiary is presently residing   (Apt. No.)   (Number and street)   (Town or city)   (Province or State)   (ZIP Code)

26. (a) Beneficiary's address abroad (if any) is: (Number and Street)   (Town or City)   (Province)   (Country)

    (b) If the beneficiary's native alphabet is other than Roman letters, write his/her name and address in the native alphabet:
    (Name)   (Number and Street)   (Town or City)   (Province)   (Country)

27. If this petition is for a child, (a). is the child married?_____ (b). is the child your adopted child? _____ If so, give the names, dates, and places of birth of all other children adopted by you. If none, so state.

28. If this petition is for a brother or sister, are both your parents the same as the alien's parents? _____ If not, submit a separate statement giving full details as to parentage, dates of marriage of parents, and the number of previous marriages of each parent

29. If separate petitions are also being submitted for other relatives, give names of each and relationship to petitioner

30. Have you ever filed a petition for this alien before? _____ If so, give place and date of filing and result.

31. If beneficiary is in the United States, give the following information concerning beneficiary

    (a) Last arrived in U.S. as _____
    (Visitor, student, exchange alien, crewman, stowaway, etc.) on (Month) (Day) (Year)

    (b) Date beneficiary's stay expired or will expire as shown on his Form I-94 or I-95. (Month) (Day) (Year)

    (c) Beneficiary's File number if any A-

    (d) Name and address of present employer

    (e) Date alien began this employment

I-130   Page 2

187

UNITED STATES DEPARTMENT OF JUSTICE
Immigration and Naturalization Service

Form approved
OMB No. 43–R123

AFFIDAVIT OF SUPPORT

(ANSWER ALL ITEMS; FILL IN WITH TYPEWRITER OR PRINT IN BLOCK LETTERS IN INK.)

I, _____, residing at _____
     (Name)   (Street and Number)

_____ _____ _____ _____
(City)   (State)   (ZIP Code if in U.S.)   (Country)

BEING DULY SWORN DEPOSE AND SAY:

1. I was born on _____ at _____
             (Date)   (City)   (Country)

If you are not a native born United States citizen, answer the following as appropriate:
   a. If a United States citizen through naturalization, give certificate of naturalization number _____
   b. If a United States citizen through parent(s) or marriage, give citizenship certificate number _____
   c. If United States citizenship was derived by some other method, attach a statement of explanation.
   d. If a lawfully admitted permanent resident of the United States, give 'A' number _____
2. That I am _____ years of age and have resided in the United States since (date) _____
3. That this affidavit is executed in behalf of the following person:

_____   _____   _____
(Name)   (Sex)   (Age)

_____ _____ _____
(Citizen of — Country)   (Marital Status)   (Relationship to Deponent)

_____ _____ _____ _____
(Presently resides at — Street and Number) (City)   (State)   (Country)

4. That this affidavit is made by me for the purpose of assuring the United States Government that the person named in item 3 will not become a public charge in the United States.

5. That I am willing and able to receive, maintain and support the person named in item 3. That I am ready and willing to deposit a bond, if necessary, to guarantee that such person will not become a public charge during his or her stay in the United States, or to guarantee that the above named will maintain his or her nonimmigrant status if admitted temporarily and will depart prior to the expiration of his or her authorized stay in the United States.

6. That I understand this affidavit will be binding upon me for a period of three (3) years after entry of the person named in item 3 and that the information and documenation provided by me may be made available to the Secretary of Health and Human Services.

7. That I am employed as, or engaged in the business of _____ with _____
                                       (Type of business)   (Name of concern)

at _____
   (Street and Number)   (City)   (State)   (ZIP Code)

I derive an annual income of (if self-employed, I have attached a copy of my last income tax return or report of commercial rating concern which I certify to be true and correct to the best of my knowledge and belief. See instruction for nature of evidence of net worth to be submitted.) $_____

I have on deposit in savings banks in the United States $_____

I have other personal property, the reasonable value of which is $_____

I have stocks and bonds with the following market value, as indicated on the attached list which I certify to be true and correct to the best of my knowledge and belief. $_____

I have life insurance in the sum of $_____
With a cash surrender value of $_____

I own real estate valued at $_____
With mortgages or other encumbrances thereon amounting to $_____
Which is located at _____
   (Street and number)   (City)   (State)   (ZIP Code)

Form I-134
(Rev. 9–30–80) N

I-134   Affidavit of Support

188

8. That the following persons are dependent upon me for support: (Place a check ✓ in the appropriate column to indicate whether the person named is wholly or partially dependent upon you for support.)

NAME OF PERSON	WHOLLY DEPENDENT	PARTIALLY DEPENDENT	AGE	RELATIONSHIP TO ME

9. That I have previously submitted affidavit(s) of support for the following person(s). If none, state none.

Name   *Date submitted*

_____   _____

_____   _____

_____   _____

10. That I have submitted visa petition(s) to the Immigration and Naturalization Service on behalf of the following person(s). If none, state none.

Name   *Relationship*   *Date submitted*

_____

_____

11. (Complete this block only if the person named in item 3 will be in the United States temporarily.) That I ☐ do intend ☐ do not intend, to make specific contributions to the support of the person named in item 3. (If you check "do intend", indicate the exact nature and duration of the contributions. For example, if you intend to furnish room and board, state for how long and, if money, state the amount in United States dollars and state whether it is to be given in a lump sum, weekly, or monthly, and for how long.)

_____

_____

OATH OR AFFIRMATION OF DEPONENT

I swear (affirm) that I know the contents of this affidavit signed by me and the statements are true and correct.

Signature of deponent _____

Subscribed and sworn to (affirmed) before me this _____ *day of* _____ , 19 _____

at _____ . *My commission expires on* _____ .

Signature of Officer Administering Oath _____ *Title* _____

If affidavit prepared by other than deponent, please complete the following:
I declare that this document was prepared by me at the request of the deponent and is based on all information of which I have any knowledge.

_____   _____   _____
(Signature)   *(Address)*   *(Date)*

I-134   Page 2

FORM I-140
(Rev. 6-20-80) N

UNITED STATES DEPARTMENT OF JUSTICE
IMMIGRATION AND NATURALIZATION SERVICE

Form approved
OMB No. 43—R0418

PETITION TO CLASSIFY PREFERENCE STATUS OF ALIEN ON BASIS OF PROFESSION OR OCCUPATION

DATE RECEIVED	FEE STAMP

TO THE SECRETARY OF STATE

Petition was filed on _____

Beneficiary's file number: A_____
Petition is approved for status under section ☐ 203(a)(3). ☐ 203(a)(6)

☐ Sec. 212(a)(14) certification attached.

☐ Blanket Sec. 212(a)(14) certification issued.

DATE
OF
ACTION

DD

DISTRICT

REMARKS

============ PETITIONER IS NOT TO WRITE ABOVE THIS LINE ============

Read this form and the attached instructions carefully before filling in petition

Petition is hereby made to classify the status of the alien beneficiary named herein for issuance of an immigrant visa as ("X" one)

☐ A THIRD PREFERENCE IMMIGRANT—An alien who is a member of the professions, or who because of his exceptional ability in the sciences or arts will substantially benefit prospectively the national economy, cultural interests or welfare of the United States, and whose services are sought by an employer. (Sec. 203(a)(3), Immigration and Nationality Act, as amended.)

☐ A SIXTH PREFERENCE IMMIGRANT—An alien who is capable of performing skilled or unskilled labor, not of a temporary or seasonal nature, for which a shortage of employable and willing persons exists in the United States. (Sec. 203 (a) (6), Immigration and Nationality Act, as amended.)

(If you need more space to answer fully any questions on this form, use a separate sheet, identify each answer with the number of the corresponding question and sign and date each sheet.)

PART I— INFORMATION CONCERNING ALIEN BENEFICIARY

1. NAME (Last, in CAPS) (First) (Middle)	2. ALIEN REGISTRATION NO. (If any)	3. PROFESSION OR OCCUPATION
4. OTHER NAMES USED (Married woman give maiden name)	5. DO NOT WRITE IN THIS SPACE	6. DOES BENEFICIARY INTEND TO ENGAGE IN HIS/HER PROFESSION OR OCCUPATION IN THE UNITED STATES? ☐ YES ☐ NO. IF "NO," EXPLAIN.
7. PLACE OF BIRTH (Country)	8. DATE OF BIRTH (Month, day, year)	
9. NAME OF PETITIONER (Full name of organization; if petitioner is an individual give full name with last in capital letters)		10. NUMBER OF YEARS OF BENEFICIARY'S EXPERIENCE (If none explain why.)

11. CITY AND STATE IN THE UNITED STATES WHERE ALIEN INTENDS TO RESIDE

_____ _____
(City) (State)

12. BENEFICIARY'S PRESENT ADDRESS (Number and street) (City or town) (State or province) (Country) (ZIP Code, if in U.S.)

13. TO YOUR KNOWLEDGE, HAS A VISA PETITION EVER BEEN FILED BY OR ON BEHALF OF THIS BENEFICIARY BASED ON HIS/HER PROFESSION OR OCCUPATION? ☐ Yes ☐ No. If "Yes," give name of each petitioner and date and place of filing.

14. IF BENEFICIARY IS NOW IN THE U.S. (a) HE/SHE LAST ARRIVED ON _____
(Month) (Day) (Year)

AS A _____ (b) SHOW DATE BENEFICIARY'S STAY EXPIRED OR WILL EXPIRE AS
(Visitor, student, exchange alien, temporary worker, crewman, stowaway, etc.)
SHOWN ON FORM I-94 OR I-95 (Show latest date)_____

15. BENEFICIARY'S SPOUSE (If Unmarried, State Unmarried)	NAME (Last name) (First name) (Middle name) (Maiden name, if married woman)			
	COUNTRY OF BIRTH	DATE OF BIRTH	PRESENT ADDRESS (No. and Street) (City or town) (State or Province) (Country)	
16. BENEFICIARY'S CHILDREN (If None State None)	NAME (Show M or S for married or single)	M.S.	BIRTHDATE	COUNTRY OF BIRTH	ADDRESS

	RECEIVED	TRANS. IN	RET'D-TRANS. OUT	COMPLETED

I-140 — Petition to Classify Preference Status of Alien on Basis of Profession or Occupation

190

17. "X" THE APPROPRIATE BOX BELOW AND FURNISH THE INFORMATION REQUIRED FOR THE BOX MARKED

☐ Alien will apply for a visa abroad at the American Consulate in _____ _____
    (City in foreign country)   (Foreign country)

☐ Alien is in the United States and will apply for adjustment of status to that of a lawful permanent resident in the office of the Immigration and
    Naturalization Service at _____ _____ If the application for adjustment of status is denied
    (City)   (State)

    the alien will apply for a visa abroad at the American Consulate in _____ _____
    (City in foreign country)   (Foreign country)

PART II—INFORMATION CONCERNING EMPLOYER AND POSITION

18. NAME OF PETITIONER (Full name of organization; if petitioner is an individual give full name with last in capital letters)

19. ADDRESS   (Number and street)   (Town or city)   (State)   (ZIP code)

20. PETITIONER IS (X one)
    ☐ U.S. CITIZEN   ☐ PERMANENT RESIDENT ALIEN (A NUMBER _____)   ☐ NONIMMIGRANT   ☐ ORGANIZATION

21. NET ANNUAL INCOME   22. WILL BENEFICIARY BE EMPLOYED AT THE ABOVE ADDRESS?   ☐ YES ☐ NO   IF NO GIVE ADDRESS
                              WHERE THE ALIEN WILL WORK.

23. DO YOU DESIRE AND INTEND TO EMPLOY THE BENEFICIARY   ☐ YES ☐ NO

24. HAVE YOU EVER FILED A VISA PETITION FOR AN ALIEN BASED ON PROFESSION OR OCCUPATION?   ☐ YES ☐ NO   IF YES, HOW
    MANY SUCH PETITIONS HAVE YOU FILED?

25. ARE SEPARATE PETITIONS BEING SUBMITTED AT THIS TIME FOR OTHER ALIENS?   ☐ YES ☐ NO   IF YES, GIVE NAME OF EACH ALIEN

26. THE FOLLOWING DOCUMENTS ARE SUBMITTED WITH THIS PETITION AND ARE MADE A PART THEREOF.

PART III—OATH OR AFFIRMATION OF PETITIONER OR AUTHORIZED REPRESENTATIVE

27. This petition was prepared by ("X" one)   ☐ the petitioner   ☐ another person
    If petition was prepared by another person, Item 29 below must also be completed
    The petition may be subscribed and sworn to or affirmed by the following persons
    In third preference cases — by the beneficiary or by the person filing the petition on the beneficiary's behalf. If the petition is being filed by a person on
    behalf of the alien beneficiary, Item 28 below must be completed by that person
    In sixth preference cases — by the employer who desires and intends to employ the beneficiary. If the employer is an organization the petition must be signed, sub-
    scribed and sworn to or affirmed by a high level officer or employee of the organization

I swear (affirm) that I have examined the contents of this petition and the accompanying documents and that the statements in this petition and the accompanying
documents are true and correct to the best of my information and belief

*If petitioner is an organization, print full name and title of autho-
rized official who is signing petition in behalf of organization:*   SIGNATURE _____
                                                                        (Petitioner's full, true, and correct name)

Name and Title _____

Subscribed and sworn to (affirmed) before me this _____ , day of _____ 19_____

at _____

[SEAL]   My commission expires _____
                                    (Signature of officer administering oath)   (Title)

28.   DECLARATION OF PERSON FILING PETITION FOR THIRD PREFERENCE ON BEHALF OF ALIEN BENEFICIARY

I declare that I have been requested and authorized by the alien beneficiary to file this petition on his their behalf

_____   _____   _____
(Signature)   (Address—Number, Street, City, State and ZIP Code)   (Date)

29.   SIGNATURE OF PERSON PREPARING FORM, IF OTHER THAN PETITIONER

I declare that this document was prepared by me at the request of the petitioner and is based on all information of which I have any knowledge

_____   _____   _____
(Signature)   (Address—Number, Street, City, State and ZIP Code)   (Date)

TO PETITIONER: DO NOT FILL IN THIS BLOCK — FOR USE OF IMMIGRATION OFFICER

a. Corrections numbered (   ) to (   ) were made by me or at my request

_____   _____   _____
                                              (Date)   (City)

_____   _____
(Signature of petitioner or authorized member of petitioner's organization)   (Title)

b. The person whose signature appears immediately above was interviewed under oath and affirmed all allegations contained herein

_____   _____   _____
(Date)   (City)   (Signature and Title)

I-140   Page 2

APPLICATION FOR STATUS AS PERMANENT RESIDENT

Form Approved
O.M.B. No. 43—R0400

FEE STAMP	File No.

APPLICATION FOR THE BENEFITS OF SECTION:

☐ Sec. 203(a)(7) and Sec. 245, I&N Act   ☐ Sec. 245, I&N Act

☐ Sec. 214(d), I&N Act   ☐ Sec. 249 I&N Act

☐ Sec. 13, Act of 9/11/57

(DO NOT WRITE ABOVE THIS LINE.) (SEE INSTRUCTIONS BEFORE FILLING IN APPLICATION. IF YOU NEED MORE SPACE TO ANSWER FULLY ANY QUESTION ON THIS FORM, USE A SEPARATE SHEET AND IDENTIFY EACH ANSWER WITH THE NUMBER OF THE CORRESPONDING QUESTION. FILL IN WITH TYPEWRITER OR PRINT IN BLOCK LETTERS IN INK.)

1. I hereby apply for the status of a lawful permanent resident alien on the following basis: (Check box A, B, C, D, E, or F)

A. ☐ As a refugee to whom an immigrant visa is immediately available (Section 203(a)(7) and Section 245, I&N Act).

B. ☐ As a person who entered the U.S. with a visa issued to me as the fiancee or fiance of a U.S. citizen whom I married within 90 days after my entry, or as a child of such fiancee or fiance (Sec. 214(d), I&N Act).

C. ☐ As a former government official, or as a member of the immediate family of such official (Section 13, Act of September 11, 1957).

D. ☐ As a person to whom an immigrant visa is immediately available, other than one described above (Section 245, I&N Act).

E. ☐ As a person who has resided in the United States continuously since prior to July 1, 1924 (Section 249, I&N Act).

F. ☐ As a person who has resided in the United States continuously since a date on or after July 1, 1924, but before June 30, 1948 (Section 249, I&N Act).

2. My name is   (Last in capital letters)   (First Name)   (Middle Name)

3. Sex   ☐ Male   ☐ Female   Phone number

4. I reside in the United States at: (c/o) (No. and Street) (Apt. No.) (City) (State) (ZIP Code)

5. Have you ever applied before for permanent resident status in the U.S.? ☐ Yes ☐ No
(If "Yes", give the date and place of filing and final disposition.)

6. My alien registration number is

7. I am a citizen of (Country)

8. Date of Birth

9. Place of Birth (City or Town)   (County, Province, or State)   (Country)

10. Name as appears on nonimmigrant document (Form I-94)

I last arrived in the United States at the port of (City and State)   on (Month) (Day) (Year)   by   (Name of vessel or other means of travel)

as a (visitor, student, crewman, parolee, etc.)   my I—94 permit number is   I ☐ was ☐ was not inspected.

11. My nonimmigrant visa, number _____, was issued by the United States Consul at (City)(Country) on (Month) (Day)(Year)

12. I am ☐ single ☐ married ☐ divorced ☐ widowed

13. I have been married _____ times, including my present marriage, if now married. (If you are now married give the following:)
a. Number of times my husband or wife has been married   b. Name of husband or wife (Wife give maiden name)

c. My husband or wife resides ☐ with me ☐ apart from me at Address (Apt. No.)(No. & Street)(Town or City)(Province or State)(Country)

14. a. I have _____ sons or daughters as follows: (Complete all columns as to each son or daughter; if living with you state "with me" in last column; otherwise give city and state or country of son's or daughter's residence).

Name	Sex	Place of Birth	Date of Birth	Now living at

b. The following members of my family are also applying for permanent resident status:

15. I list below all organizations, societies, clubs, and associations, past or present, in which I have held membership in the United States or a foreign country, and the periods and places of such membership. (If you have never been a member of any organization, state "None".)

UNITED STATES DEPARTMENT OF JUSTICE
Immigration and Naturalization Service
Form I-485 (Rev. 1-10-77) N

RECEIVED	TRANS. IN	RET'D-TRANS. OUT	COMPLETED

(Page 1)

I-485   Application for Status as Permanent Resident

16. I ☐ have ☐ have not been treated for a mental disorder, drug addiction or alcoholism. (If you have been, explain.)

17. I ☐ have ☐ have not been arrested, convicted or confined in a prison. (If you have been, explain.)

18. I ☐ have ☐ have not been the beneficiary of a pardon, amnesty, rehabilitation decree, other act of clemency or similiar action. (If you have been, explain.)

19. APPLICANTS FOR STATUS AS PERMANENT RESIDENTS MUST ESTABLISH THAT THEY ARE ADMISSIBLE TO THE UNITED STATES. EXCEPT AS OTHERWISE PROVIDED BY LAW, ALIENS WITHIN ANY OF THE FOLLOWING CLASSES ARE NOT ADMISSIBLE TO THE UNITED STATES AND ARE THEREFORE INELIGIBLE FOR STATUS AS PERMANENT RESIDENTS:

Aliens who have committed or who have been convicted of a crime involving moral turpitude (does not include minor traffic violations); aliens who have been engaged in or who intend to engage in any commercialized sexual activity; aliens who are or at any time have been, anarchists, or members of or affiliated with any Communist or other totalitarian party, including any subdivision or affiliate thereof; aliens who have advocated or taught, either by personal utterance, or by means of any written or printed matter, or through affiliation with an organization, (i) opposition to organized government, (ii) the overthrow of government by force or violence, (iii) the assaulting or killing of government officials because of their official character, (iv) the unlawful destruction of property, (v) sabotage, or (vi) the doctrines of world communism, or the establishment of a totalitarian dictatorship in the United States; aliens who intend to engage in prejudicial activities or unlawful activities of a subversive nature; aliens who have been convicted of violation of any law or regulation relating to narcotic drugs or marihuana, or who have been illicit traffickers in narcotic drugs or marihuana; aliens who have been involved in assisting any other aliens to enter the United States in violation of law; aliens who have applied for exemption or discharge from training or service in the Armed Forces of the United States on the ground of alienage and who have been relieved or discharged from such training or service; medical graduates (other than those for whom Relative petitions have been approved) coming principally to perform services as members of the medical profession, unless they have passed Parts I and II of the National Board of Medical Examiners Examination (or an equivalent examination as determined by the Secretary of Health, Education, and Welfare) and who are competent in oral and written English.

Do any of the foregoing classes apply to you? ☐ Yes ☐ No *(If answer is Yes, explain)*

20. *(COMPLETE THIS BLOCK ONLY IF YOU CHECKED BOX "A", "B", "C", or "D" OF BLOCK 1)*

APPLICANTS WHO CHECKED BOX "A" "B" "C" OR "D" OF BLOCK 1 (INCLUDING REFUGEES) IN ADDITION TO ESTABLISHING THAT THEY ARE NOT MEMBERS OF ANY OF THE INADMISSIBLE CLASSES DESCRIBED IN BLOCK 10 ABOVE MUST, EXCEPT AS OTHERWISE PROVIDED BY LAW, ALSO ESTABLISH THAT THEY ARE NOT WITHIN ANY OF THE FOLLOWING INADMISSIBLE CLASSES:

Aliens who are mentally retarded, insane, or have suffered one or more attacks of insanity; aliens afflicted with psychopathic personality, sexual deviation, mental defect, narcotic drug addiction, chronic alcoholism or any dangerous contagious disease; aliens who have a physical defect, disease or disability affecting their ability to earn a living; aliens who are paupers, professional beggars or vagrants; aliens who are polygamists or advocate polygamy; aliens who intend to perform skilled or unskilled labor and who have not been certified by the Secretary of Labor (see Instruction 10); aliens likely to become a public charge; aliens who have been excluded from the United States within the past year, or who at any time have been deported from the United States, or who at any time have been removed from the United States at Government expense; aliens who have procured or have attempted to procure a visa by fraud or misrepresentation; aliens who have departed from or remained outside the United States to avoid military service in time of war or national emergency; aliens who are former exchange visitors who are subject to but have not complied with the two year foreign residence requirement.

Do any of the foregoing classes apply to you? ☐ Yes ☐ No *(If answer is Yes, explain)*

21. I ☐ do ☐ do not intend to seek gainful employment in the United States. If you intend to seek gainful employment in the United States, state the occupation you intend to follow_____

I-485   Page 2

22. *(Complete this block only if you checked box A or D of block 1)*

☐ a. I have a priority on the consular waiting list at the American Consulate at _____ as of _____
(City)   (Date)

☐ b. A visa petition according me ☐ immediate relative ☐ preference status was approved by the district

director at _____ on _____
(City and State)   (Date)

☐ c. A visa petition has not been approved in my behalf but I claim eligibility for preference status because ☐ my spouse

☐ my parent is the beneficiary of a visa petition approved by the district director at _____
(City and State)

on _____
(Date)

☐ d. I am claiming preference status as a refugee under the proviso to Section 203 (a)(7) of the Act who has been continuously physically present in the United States for at least the past two years. *(If you check this item, you must execute and attach Form I 590A to this application.)*

☐ e. Other *(Explain)*

23. *(Complete this block only if you checked Box E or F of Block 1)*

A. I first arrived in the United States at (Port) _____

on (Date) _____

by means of (Name of vessel or other means of travel) _____

I ☐ was ☐ was not inspected by an immigration officer.

B. I entered the U.S. under the name *(Name at time of entry)* _____

and I was destined to (City and State) _____

I was coming to join (Name and relationship) _____

C. Since my first entry I ☐ have ☐ have not been absent from the United States. *(If you have been absent, attach a separate statement listing the port, date and means of each departure from and return to the U. S.)*

24. ☐ Completed Form G—325A (Biographic Information) is attached as part of this application.   ☐ Completed Form G—325A (Biographic Information) is not attached as applicant is under 14 years of age.

25. IF YOUR NATIVE ALPHABET IS IN OTHER THAN ROMAN LETTERS, WRITE YOUR NAME IN YOUR NATIVE ALPHABET BELOW:

Signature of Applicant:

Date of Signature:

26. (Signature of person preparing form, if other than applicant.) I declare that this document was prepared by me at the request of the applicant and is based on all information on which I have any knowledge.

Address of person preparing form, if other than applicant

Date:

Occupation:

(Application not to be signed below until applicant appears before an officer of the Immigration and Naturalization Service for examination)

I, _____, do swear (affirm) that I know the contents of this application subscribed by me including the attached documents, that the same are true to the best of my knowledge, and that corrections numbered ( ) to ( ) were made by me or at my request, and that this application was signed by me with my full, true name:

_____
(Complete and true signature of applicant)

Subscribed and sworn to before me by the above-named applicant at _____ on _____
(Month) (Day) (Year)

_____
(Signature and title of officer)

(Page 3)

I-485   Page 3

Form Approved
OMB No. 43-R0342

UNITED STATES DEPARTMENT OF JUSTICE
IMMIGRATION AND NATURALIZATION SERVICE

Fee Stamp

APPLICATION FOR CHANGE
OF NONIMMIGRANT STATUS
(Under Section 248 of the Immigration and Nationality Act)

➡ **Please read the instructions on the first page**

I hereby apply to have my status in the United States changed to that of a nonimmigrant_____
(Student, visitor, etc.)

I wish to remain in the United States in that new status until_____
(Month, Day, Year)

This application is submitted together with the required documents which are made a part hereof and, if applicable, the fee of $10.

PRESS FIRMLY–LEGIBLE COPY REQUIRED. PRINT OR TYPE YOUR NAME EXACTLY AS IT APPEARS ON YOUR ARRIVAL-DEPARTURE RECORD FORM I-94. IF YOUR MAILING ADDRESS IN THE U. S. IS WITH SOMEONE WHOSE FAMILY NAME IS DIFFERENT FROM YOURS, INSERT THAT PERSON'S NAME IN THE C/O BLOCK.

1. YOUR NAME	FAMILY NAME (Capital Letters)	GIVEN	MIDDLE
IN CARE OF	C/O	FILE NUMBER (If Known)	
2. MAILING ADDRESS IN U.S.	NUMBER AND STREET (Apt. No.)		
	CITY	STATE	ZIP CODE
3. DATE OF BIRTH (Month, Day, Year)	COUNTRY OF BIRTH	COUNTRY OF CITIZENSHIP	
4. PRESENT NONIMMIGRANT CLASSIFICATION	DATE ON WHICH AUTHORIZED STAY EXPIRES		
5. DATE AND PORT OF LAST ARRIVAL IN UNITED STATES	NAME OF VESSEL, AIRLINE, OR OTHER MEANS OF LAST ARRIVAL IN U.S.		

6. I AM IN POSSESSION OF PASSPORT

NUMBER:*
ISSUED BY (Country)

WHICH EXPIRES ON: (Month, Day, Year)

7. MY I-94 IS ATTACHED ☐ YES ☐ NO
If "No", it was ☐ Lost ☐ Stolen ☐ Destroyed
☐ Other (Specify)_____

8. I ENTERED WITH *NONIMMIGRANT VISA NO.

9. MY NONIMMIGRANT STATUS IN THE UNITED
STATES ☐ HAS ☐ HAS NOT BEEN CHANGED
SINCE MY ENTRY (if changed, give details)

Reclassification   FOR GOVERNMENT USE ONLY
to
☐ STAY GRANTED TO (Date)   DATE OF ACTION

☐ Application DENIED. V.D. TO (Date)   DD OR OIC OFFICE

10. MY PERMANENT ADDRESS OUTSIDE THE UNITED STATES IS: (Street) (City or Town) (County, District, Province or State) (Country)

11. I RESIDED AT THE ADDRESS IN ITEM 10 FROM: (Month, Day, Year)   TO: (Month, Day, Year)

12. SINCE MY ENTRY INTO THE UNITED STATES, I HAVE RESIDED AT THE FOLLOWING PLACES:

(Street and No.) (City or Town) (State)	FROM: (Month, Day, Year)	TO: (Month, Day, Year)
		Present Time

13. I DESIRE TO HAVE MY NONIMMIGRANT STATUS CHANGED FOR THE FOLLOWING REASONS:

14. I DID NOT APPLY TO THE AMERICAN CONSUL FOR A VISA IN THE NONIMMIGRANT STATUS WHICH I AM NOW SEEKING FOR THE FOLLOWING REASONS:

15. I SUBMIT THE FOLLOWING DOCUMENTARY EVIDENCE TO ESTABLISH THAT I WILL MAINTAIN THE NONIMMIGRANT CLASSIFICATION TO WHICH I WISH TO BE CHANGED:

ATTACH YOUR FORM I-94 *DO NOT SEND YOUR PASSPORT

RECEIVED	TRANS. IN	RETO. TRANS OUT	COMPLETED

FORM I-506 (REV. 10-22-...)

I-506   Application for Change of Nonimmigrant Status

16. (COMPLETE THIS BLOCK ONLY IF YOU ARE APPLYING FOR CHANGE TO STUDENT STATUS.)
THE COUNTRY IN WHICH I INTEND TO LIVE AND WORK AFTER I COMPLETE MY SCHOOLING IN THE UNITED STATES IS_____

(IF YOU ARE SEEKING TO ATTEND A VOCATIONAL OR BUSINESS SCHOOL, COMPLETE THE FOLLOWING ADDITIONAL STATEMENTS BY CHECKING THE APPROPRIATE BOXES.)
THE SCHOOLING I AM SEEKING ☐ IS ☐ IS NOT AVAILABLE IN MY COUNTRY.

I ☐ INTEND ☐ DO NOT INTEND TO ENGAGE IN THE OCCUPATION FOR WHICH THAT SCHOOLING WILL PREPARE ME.

17. MY OCCUPATION IS:

18. SOCIAL SECURITY NO. (If none, state "none")

19. I ☐ HAVE ☐ HAVE NOT BEEN EMPLOYED OR ENGAGED IN BUSINESS SINCE ENTERING THE UNITED STATES. IF ANSWER IS IN AFFIRMATIVE, COMPLETE THE FOLLOWING:
NATURE OF OCCUPATION OR BUSINESS IN WHICH I ☐ AM ☐ WAS EMPLOYED:

NAME OF EMPLOYER OR BUSINESS FIRM   ADDRESS

MY EMPLOYMENT OR ENGAGEMENT IN BUSINESS BEGAN ON: (Month, Day, Year)   AND ENDED ON: (Month, Day, Year)

MY MONTHLY INCOME FROM EMPLOYMENT OR BUSINESS ☐ IS ☐ WAS: $

20. IF NOT EMPLOYED OR ENGAGED IN BUSINESS IN THE UNITED STATES, DESCRIBE FULLY THE SOURCE AND AMOUNT OF YOUR INCOME ABROAD AND HOW SUPPORTED WHILE IN THE UNITED STATES: (If applying for change to student status, see Instruction # 4.)

21. I ☐ AM ☐ AM NOT MARRIED

Name of Spouse	Present address of Spouse	Citizenship (Country) of Spouse

22. I HAVE_____(Number) CHILDREN: (List children below)

Name	Age	Place of Birth	Present Address

23. I HAVE_____(Number) RELATIVES IN THE UNITED STATES OTHER THAN MY SPOUSE AND/OR CHILDREN: (List relatives below)

Name	Relationship	Immigration Status	Present Address

24. I ☐ HAVE ☐ HAVE NOT SUBMITTED THE ADDRESS REPORTS REQUIRED BY THE ALIEN REGISTRATION ACT OF 1940, AS AMENDED, AND BY SECTION 265 OF THE IMMIGRATION AND NATIONALITY ACT.

25. I ☐ HAVE ☐ HAVE NOT BEEN ARRESTED OR CONVICTED OF ANY CRIMINAL OFFENSE IN THE UNITED STATES OR IN ANY FOREIGN COUNTRY. IF ANSWER IS IN THE AFFIRMATIVE, GIVE DETAILS:

26. I certify that the above is true and correct to the best of my knowledge and belief. (If form prepared by other than applicant, that person must execute item 27.)

_____(Signature of Applicant)   (Date)

SIGNATURE OF PERSON PREPARING FORM, IF OTHER THAN APPLICANT

27. I declare that this document was prepared by me at the request of the applicant and is based on all information of which I have any knowledge.

(Signature)   (Address)   (Date)

I-506   Page 2

UNITED STATES DEPARTMENT OF JUSTICE
IMMIGRATION AND NATURALIZATION SERVICE

READ INSTRUCTIONS CAREFULLY
FEE WILL NOT BE REFUNDED

Form Approved
OMB 43-R0068

FEE STAMP

APPLICATION TO EXTEND
TIME OF TEMPORARY STAY

I HEREBY APPLY TO EXTEND MY
TEMPORARY STAY IN THE UNITED STATES

PRESS FIRMLY—LEGIBLE COPY REQUIRED. PRINT OR TYPE YOUR NAME EXACTLY AS IT APPEARS ON YOUR ARRIVAL—DEPARTURE RECORD FORM I-94. IF YOUR MAILING ADDRESS IN THE U.S. IS WITH SOMEONE WHOSE FAMILY NAME IS DIFFERENT FROM YOURS, INSERT THAT PERSON'S NAME IN THE C/O BLOCK.

6. DATE TO WHICH EXTENSION IS REQUESTED

1. YOUR NAME | FAMILY NAME (CAPITAL LETTERS) | FIRST | MIDDLE

7. REASON FOR REQUESTING EXTENSION

IN CARE OF | C/O

2. MAILING ADDRESS IN U.S. | NUMBER AND STREET (APT. NO.) | FILE NUMBER
CITY | STATE | ZIP CODE

3. DATE OF BIRTH (MO./DAY/YR.) | COUNTRY OF BIRTH | COUNTRY OF CITIZENSHIP

4. PRESENT NONIMMIGRANT CLASSIFICATION | DATE ON WHICH AUTHORIZED STAY EXPIRES

5. DATE AND PORT OF LAST ARRIVAL IN U.S. | NAME OF VESSEL, AIRLINE, OR OTHER MEANS OF LAST ARRIVAL IN U.S.

8. REASON FOR COMING TO THE U.S.

FOR GOVERNMENT USE ONLY

☐ EXTENSION GRANTED TO (DATE) | DATE OF ACTION

9. HAS AN IMMIGRANT VISA PETITION EVER BEEN FILED IN YOUR BEHALF?
☐ YES ☐ NO IF "YES", WHERE WAS IT FILED?

☐ EXTENSION DENIED V.D. TO (DATE) | DD OR OIC OFFICE

10. HAVE YOU EVER APPLIED FOR AN IMMIGRANT VISA OR PERMANENT RESIDENCE IN THE U.S.? ☐ YES ☐ NO IF "YES", WHERE DID YOU APPLY?

11. I INTEND TO DEPART FROM THE U.S. ON (DATE)
I AM IN POSSESSION OF A TRANSPORTATION TICKET FOR MY DEPARTURE ☐ YES ☐ ☐ NO

12. PASSPORT NO. * | EXPIRES ON (DATE) | ISSUED BY (COUNTRY) | 13. NUMBER, STREET, CITY, PROVINCE (STATE) AND COUNTRY OF PERMANENT RESIDENCE

14. MY USUAL OCCUPATION IS: | 15. SOCIAL SECURITY NO. (IF NONE, STATE "NONE")

16. I ☐ AM ☐ AM NOT MARRIED. IF YOU WISH TO APPLY FOR EXTENSION FOR YOUR SPOUSE & CHILDREN, GIVE THE FOLLOWING: (SEE INSTRUCTIONS #1)

NAME OF SPOUSE AND CHILDREN | DATE OF BIRTH | COUNTRY OF BIRTH | PASSPORT ISSUED BY (COUNTRY) AND EXPIRES ON (DATE)

NOTE IF SPOUSE AND CHILDREN FOR WHOM YOU ARE SEEKING EXTENSION DO NOT RESIDE WITH YOU, GIVE THEIR COMPLETE ADDRESS ON A SEPARATE ATTACHMENT TO THIS APPLICATION.

17. I (INSERT "HAVE" OR "HAVE NOT") .... BEEN EMPLOYED OR ENGAGED IN BUSINESS IN THE UNITED STATES. (IF YOU HAVE BEEN EMPLOYED OR ENGAGED IN BUSINESS IN THE UNITED STATES, COMPLETE THE REST OF THE BLOCK.)

NAME AND ADDRESS OF EMPLOYER OR BUSINESS | INCOME PER WEEK | DATES EMPLOYMENT OR BUSINESS BEGAN & ENDED

I certify that the above is true and correct
SIGNATURE OF APPLICANT | DATE

SIGNATURE OF PERSON PREPARING FORM, IF OTHER THAN APPLICANT

I declare that this document was prepared by me at the request of the applicant and is based on all information on which I have any knowledge.
SIGNATURE | ADDRESS | DATE

ATTACH YOUR FORM I-94 OR I-144 —*DO NOT SEND YOUR PASSPORT | RECEIVED | TRANS IN | RET'D-TRANS OUT | COMPLETED

Form I-539 (Rev. 10-15-80)N

I-539   Application to Extend Time of Temporary Stay

Form approved.
OMB No. 43-R0075

UNITED STATES DEPARTMENT OF JUSTICE
Immigration and Naturalization Service

ALIEN REGISTRATION NO. _____

APPLICATION TO FILE DECLARATION OF INTENTION

Take or Mail to—
IMMIGRATION AND NATURALIZATION SERVICE,

Date _____ , 19 ____

(TO APPLICANT.-Read carefully and follow the instructions on page 2)

(1) My full name is _____
(Full, true name, without abbreviation and any other name which has been used, must appear here)

(2) My place of residence is _____
(Apt. No.)   (Number and street)   (City or town)   (County)   (State)   (ZIP Code)

(3) I was born on _____ , in _____
(Month)   (Day)   (Year)

_____
(City or town)   (County, district, province or State)   (Country)

(4) I ☐ am ☐ am not married; the name of my wife or husband is _____

_____

(5) My lawful admission for permanent residence in the United States was at _____
(City or town)   (State)

under the name of _____ on _____
(Month)   (Day)   (Year)

and I arrived on _____
(Name of vessel or other conveyance)

(6) Since my lawful admission for permanent residence I have not been absent from the United States for a period or periods of six months or longer, except as follows:

DEPARTED FROM THE UNITED STATES			RETURNED TO THE UNITED STATES		
Port	Date (Month, day, year)	Vessel or Other Means of Conveyance	Port	Date (Month, day, year)	Vessel or Other Means of Conveyance

(7) My father's full name is/was _____

(8) My mother' maiden name was _____

(9) I desire to declare my intention to become a citizen of the United States in the _____
(Name of court)

Court at _____
(City or town)   (State)

I CERTIFY that the above statement of facts is true to the best of my knowledge and belief.

Signature of person preparing form, if other than applicant. | Signature of Applicant

I declare that this document was prepared by me at the request of applicant and is based on all information of which I have any knowledge.
Signature | Address at Which Applicant Receives Mail   (Street)   (City)

Address: | Date: | (State)   (ZIP Code)

Form N-300
(Rev.10-15-79)N

(OVER)

GPO 945-008

N-300   Application to File Declaration of Intention

198

INSTRUCTIONS TO APPLICANT

1. *A declaration of intention is not required for the purpose of filing a petition for naturalization or to become a citizen of the United States. You must be over 18 years of age to file this application.*

2. Show your Alien Registration number in the box at the top of page 1.

3. PHOTOGRAPHS.—You are required to send with this application three identical photographs of yourself taken within 30 days of the date of this application. They may be in natural color or in black and white, but black and white photographs which have been tinted or otherwise colored are not acceptable. These photographs must be 2 by 2 inches in size, and the distance from top of head to point of chin should be approximately 1¼ inches. They must not be pasted on cards or mounted in any other way, must be on thin paper, have a light background, and clearly show a front view of your face without hat. Snapshots and group or full-length portraits will not be accepted. All of these photographs must be signed by you on the margin and not on the face or the clothing.

4. DATE OF YOUR ARRIVAL.—If you do not know the exact date of your arrival in the United States, or the name of the vessel or port, and you cannot obtain this information by consulting your family or friends who came over with you, give the facts of your arrival as you remember them in the appropriate blank spaces on the first page of this form. Your Immigrant Identification Card or your passport, ship's card, or baggage labels, if you have them, may help you to answer these questions.

If the date of your arrival in the United States was on or before June 29, 1906, you should submit with this application documentary evidence of your residence in the United States prior to that date. Such documents may be family Bible entries, deeds of record, wills or other authentic legal documents, life insurance policies, bank books and records, employment records or other documents showing that you entered the United States on or before June 29, 1906. Do not submit such documents if your arrival in the United States was after June 29, 1906.

5. FEE.—Please be prepared to pay a fee of five dollars ($5) when you appear before the Court Clerk for your copy of the declaration of intention.

6. Authority for collection of the information requested on this form is contained in Section 334(f) of the Immigration and Nationality Act of 1952 (8 U.S.C. 1445(f)). Submission of the information is voluntary. The purpose of requesting the information is to enable this Service to determine whether you are statutorily eligible to file a declaration of intention. The information submitted will be used to prepare a declaration of intention and to inform the clerk of the court to accept, file and issue a declaration of intention. The information solicited may, as a matter of routine use, be disclosed to other federal, state, local or foreign law enforcement and regulatory agencies, Department of Defense, including any component thereof, Selective Service System, Department of State, Department of the Treasury, Central Intelligence Agency, Interpol and individuals and organizations, during the course of investigation to elicit further information required by this Service to carry out its functions. Information solicited which indicates a violation of potential violation of law, whether civil, criminal or regulatory in nature, may be referred, as a routine use, to the appropriate agency, whether federal, state, local or foreign charged with the responsibility for investigating, enforcing or prosecuting such violations. Failure to provide any or all of the solicited information may affect approval of your application to file a declaration of intention to become a citizen of the United States.

TO APPLICANT.—Do not write below this line.

For use in searching Records of Arrival

RECORDS EXAMINED

RECORDS FOUND

Card index _____ Place _____

Index books _____ Name _____

Manifests _____ _____

_____ Date _____

_____ Manner _____

_____ Marital Status _____

TO APPLICANT.—Do not write below this line.

(Signature of person making search)

IMMIGRATION AND NATURALIZATION SERVICE.

_____, 19 ____

To Clerk of Court:

Authorization is hereby granted for the issuance of declaration of intention to the applicant named above, who has established that he is residing in the United States pursuant to a lawful admission for permanent residence, as alleged in the application.

_____ _____
(Title) (Signature)

(This form should be attached to the e declaration and returned at the end of the mor your report on Form N-4. The applicant has
been directed to appear at your office with. ays to make the declaration. If applicant does no ar within 90 days, return this form to this
Service.)

N-300   Page 2

UNITED STATES DEPARTMENT OF JUSTICE
IMMIGRATION AND NATURALIZATION SERVICE

Form Approved
OMB NO. 43-R0079

FEE STAMP

APPLICATION TO FILE PETITION FOR NATURALIZATION

Mail or take to:
IMMIGRATION AND NATURALIZATION SERVICE

ALIEN REGISTRATION

(Show the exact spelling of your name as it appears on your alien registration receipt card, and the number of your card. If you did not register, so state.)

(See INSTRUCTIONS. BE SURE YOU UNDERSTAND EACH QUESTION BEFORE YOU ANSWER IT. PLEASE PRINT OR TYPE.)

Name ....

No. ....

Section of Law ....
(Leave Blank)

Date: ....

(1) My full true and correct name is..
(Full true name without abbreviations)

(2) I now live at...
(Number and street.)

....
(City. county, state, zip code)

(3) I was born on..in...
(Month) (Day) (Year)   (City or town)   (County, province, or state)   (Country)

(4) I request that my name be changed to...

(5) Other names I have used are: ....
(Include maiden name)   Sex: ☐ Male   ☐ Female

(6) Was your father or mother ever a United States citizen?..☐ Yes ☐ No
(If "Yes", explain fully)

(7) Can you read and write English?...☐ Yes ☐ No

(8) Can you speak English?...☐ Yes ☐ No

(9) Can you sign your name in English?...☐ Yes ☐ No

(10) My lawful admission for permanent residence was on...under the name of
(Month)   (Day)   (Year)

....at...
(City)   (State)

(11) Since that date I have resided continuously in the United States and continuously in the State of.............................. where I now
live since................................ During the last five years I have been physically present in the United States for a total of..........months.

(12) Do you intend to reside permanently in the United States? ☐ Yes ☐ No If "No," explain:

(13) In what places in the United States have you lived during the last 5 years? List present address FIRST.

FROM -	To -	STREET ADDRESS	CITY AND STATE
(a) ...., 19.....	PRESENT TIME		
(b) ...., 19.....	........., 19.....		
(c) ...., 19.....	........., 19.....		
(d) ...., 19.....	........., 19.....		

(14) (a) Have you been out of the United States since your lawful admission as a permanent resident?......................☐ Yes ☐ No
If "Yes" fill in the following information for every absence of *less than 6 months*, no matter how short it was.

DATE DEPARTED	DATE RETURNED	NAME OF SHIP, OR OF AIRLINE. RAILROAD COMPANY. BUS COMPANY, OR OTHER MEANS USED TO RETURN TO THE UNITED STATES	PLACE OR PORT OF ENTRY THROUGH WHICH YOU RETURNED TO THE UNITED STATES

(b) Since your lawful admission, have you been out of the United States for a period of *6 months or longer?*..........☐ Yes ☐ No
If "No", state "None"; If "Yes", fill in following information for every absence of more than 6 months.

DATE DEPARTED	DATE RETURNED	NAME OF SHIP, OR OF AIRLINE. RAILROAD COMPANY. BUS COMPANY, OR OTHER MEANS USED TO RETURN TO THE UNITED STATES	PLACE OR PORT OF ENTRY THROUGH WHICH YOU RETURNED TO THE UNITED STATES

(OVER)

Form N-400 (Rev. 11-1-80)N

(1)

N-400   Application to File Petition for Naturalization

(2)

(15) The law provides that you may not be regarded as qualified for naturalization, if you knowingly committed certain offenses or crimes, even though you may not have been arrested. Have you ever, in or outside the United States:

(a) knowingly committed any crime for which you have not been arrested? .... □ Yes □ No

(b) been arrested, cited, charged, indicted, convicted, fined or imprisoned for breaking or violating any law or ordinance, including traffic regulations? .... □ Yes □ No

If you answer "Yes" to (a) or (b), give the following information as to each incident.

WHEN	WHERE	(City)	(State)	(Country)	NATURE OF OFFENSE	OUTCOME OF CASE, IF ANY
(a)						
(b)						
(c)						
(d)						
(e)						

(16) List your present and past membership in or affiliation with every organization, association, fund, foundation, party, club, society or similar group in the United States or in any other country or place, and your foreign military service. (If none, write "None.")

(a) ...., 19........ to 19........

(b) ...., 19........ to 19........

(c) ...., 19........ to 19........

(d) ...., 19........ to 19........

(e) ...., 19........ to 19........

(f) ...., 19........ to 19........

(g) ...., 19........ to 19........

(17) (a) Are you now, or have you ever, in the United States or in any other place, been a member of, or in any other way connected or associated with the Communist Party? (If "Yes", attach full explanation) .... □ Yes □ No

(b) Have you ever knowingly aided or supported the Communist Party directly, or indirectly through another organization, group or person? (If "Yes", attach full explanation) .... □ Yes □ No

(c) Do you now or have you ever advocated, taught, believed in, or knowingly supported or furthered the interests of Communism? (If "Yes", attach full explanation) .... □ Yes □ No

(18) Have you borne any hereditary title or have you been of any order of nobility in any foreign state? .... □ Yes □ No

(19) **Have you ever been declared legally incompetent or have you ever been confined as a patient in a mental institution?** .... □ Yes □ No

(20) Are deportation proceedings pending against you, or have you ever been deported or ordered deported, or have you ever applied for suspension of deportation? .... □ Yes □ No

(21) (a) My last Federal income tax return was filed............................ (year) Do you owe any Federal taxes? .... □ Yes □ No

(b) Since becoming a permanent resident of the United States, have you:

—filed an income tax return as a nonresident? .... □ Yes □ No

—failed to file an income tax return because you regarded yourself as a nonresident? .... □ Yes □ No

(If you answer "Yes" to (a) or (b) explain fully.)

(22) Have you ever claimed in writing, or in any other way, to be a United States citizen? .... □ Yes □ No

(23) (a) Have you ever deserted from the military, air, or naval forces of the United States? .... □ Yes □ No

(b) If male, have you ever left the United States to avoid being drafted into the Armed Forces of the United States? ...... □ Yes □ No

(24) The law provides that you may not be regarded as qualified for naturalization if, at *any* time during the period for which you are required to prove good moral character, you have been a habitual drunkard; committed adultery; advocated or practiced polygamy; have been a prostitute or procured anyone for prostitution; have knowingly and for gain helped any alien to enter the United States illegally; have been an illicit trafficker in narcotic drugs or marijuana; have received your income mostly from illegal gambling, or have given false testimony for the purpose of obtaining any benefits under this Act. Have you ever, *anywhere*, been such a person or committed any of these acts? (If you answer yes to any of these, attach full explanation.) .... □ Yes □ No

(25) Do you believe in the Constitution and form of government of the United States? .... □ Yes □ No

(26) Are you willing to bear the full oath of allegiance to the United States? (See Instructions) .... □ Yes □ No

(27) If the law requires it, are you willing:

(a) to bear arms on behalf of the United States? (If "No", attach full explanation) .... □ Yes □ No

(b) to perform noncombatant services in the Armed Forces of the United States? (If "No", attach full explanation) ....□ Yes □ No

(c) to perform work of national importance under civilian direction? (If "No", attach full explanation) .... □ Yes □ No

(28) (a) If male, did you ever register under United States Selective Service laws or draft laws? .... □ Yes □ No

If "Yes" give date................; Selective Service No.....................; Local Board No.................; Present classification..................

(b) Did you ever apply for exemption from military service because of alienage, conscientious objections, or other reasons? □ Yes □ No

If "Yes," explain fully..

(29) If serving or ever served in the Armed Forces of the United States, give branch..;

from...................., 19........ to ...., 19......., and from......................., 19....... to ...., 19.......

□ inducted or □ enlisted at..; Service No.............................;

type of discharge...; ....; rank at discharge.................................;

(Honorable, Dishonorable, etc.)

reason for discharge ....

(alienage, conscientious objector, other)

□ Reserve or □ National Guard from...... .... 19. to..................................

N-400   Page 2

(30) My occupation is..
List the names, addresses, and occupations (or types of business) of your employers during the last 5 years? (If none, write "None.")
List present employment FIRST.

FROM-	TO-	EMPLOYER'S NAME	ADDRESS	OCCUPATION OR TYPE OF BUSINESS
(a) ...., 19......	PRESENT TIME			
(b) ...., 19......	.............., 19......			
(c) ...., 19......	.............., 19......			
(d) ...., 19......	.............., 19......			

(31) Complete this block if you are or have been married.
I am.. The first name of my husband or wife is (was)..................
　　　　(Single, married, divorced, widowed)
We were married on.................................. at.. He or she was born at.........................
.... on .... He or she entered the United States at (place)...................
.... on (date).. for permanent residence and now resides ☐ with me
☐ apart from me at ....
　　　　　　　　(Show full address if not living with you.)
He or she was naturalized on..; Certificate No....................,
or became a citizen by .... His or her alien Registration No. is...

(32) How many times have you been married?........... How many times has your husband or wife been married?........... If either of you has
been married more than once, fill in the following information for each previous marriage.

DATE MARRIED	DATE MARRIAGE ENDED	NAME OF PERSON TO WHOM MARRIED	SEX	(Check One) PERSON MARRIED WAS CITIZEN☐ ALIEN☐	HOW MARRIAGE ENDED
(a)				☐ .... ☐	
(b)				☐ .... ☐	
(c)				☐ .... ☐	
(d)				☐ .... ☐	

(33) I have..............children: (Complete columns (a) to (h) as to each child. If child lives with you, state "with me" in column (h), other-
　　　　(Number)　　　　wise give city and State of child's residence.)

(a) Given Names	(b) Sex	(c) Place Born (Country)	(d) Date Born	(e) Date of Entry	(f) Port of Entry	(g) Alien Registration No.	(h) Now Living at-

(34) READ INSTRUCTION NO. 6 BEFORE ANSWERING QUESTION (36)

I..............................want certificates of citizenship for those of my children who are in the U.S. and are under age 18 years that are named below.
(Do) (Do Not)

(Enclose $15 for each child for whom you want certificates, otherwise, send no money with this application.)

....
　　　　　(Write names of children under age 18 years and who are in the U.S. for whom you want certificates)

If present spouse is not the parent of the children named above, give parent's name, date and place of naturalization, and number of marriages

....

N-400　　　Page 3

202

(4)

Signature of person preparing form, if other than applicant.	SIGNATURE OF APPLICANT
I declare that this document was prepared by me at the request of applicant and is based on all information of which I have any knowledge. SIGNATURE	ADDRESS AT WHICH APPLICANT RECEIVES MAIL
ADDRESS: DATE:	APPLICANT'S TELEPHONE NUMBER

TO   APPLICANT :   DO   NOT   FILL   IN   BLANKS   BELOW   THIS   LINE.

NOTE CAREFULLY.—This application must be sworn to before an officer of the Immigration and Naturalization Service at the time you appear before such officer for examination on this application.

AFFIDAVIT

I do swear that I know the contents of this application comprising pages 1 to 4, inclusive, and the supplemental forms thereto, No(s)..., subscribed to by me; that the same are true to the best of my knowledge and belief; that corrections numbered ( ) to ( ) were made by me or at my request; and that this application was signed by me with my full, true, and correct name, SO HELP ME GOD.

Subscribed and sworn to before me by applicant at the preliminary investigation ( ) at ....

this .... day of ...., 19.......
I certify that before verification the above applicant stated in my presence that he/she had (heard) read the foregoing application, corrections therein and supplemental form(s) and understood the contents thereof.

....
(Complete and true signature of applicant)

....
(Naturalization examiner)

(For demonstration of applicant's ability to write English)

(1st witness. Occupation) ....

(2nd witness. Occupation) ....

Nonfiled ....

....
(Date, Reasons)

NOTICE TO APPLICANTS:

Authority for collection of the information requested on this form and those forms mentioned in the instructions thereto is continued in Sections 328, 329, 332, 334, 335 or 341 of the Immigration and Nationality Act of 1952 (8 U.S.C. 1439, 1440, 1443, 1445, 1446 or 1452). Submission of the information is voluntary inasmuch as the immigration and nationality laws of the United States do not require an alien to apply for naturalization. If your Social Security number is included on a form, no right, benefit or privilege will be denied for your failure to provide such number. However, as military records are indexed by such numbers, verification of your military service, if required to establish eligibility for naturalization, may prove difficult. The principal purposes for soliciting the information are to enable designated officers of the Immigration and Naturalization Service to determine the admissibility of a petitioner for naturalization and to make appropriate recommendations to the naturalization courts. All or any part of the information solicited may, as a matter of routine use, be disclosed to a court exercising naturalization jurisdiction and to other federal, state, local or foreign law enforcement or regulatory agencies. Department of Defense, including any component thereof, the Selective Service System, the Department of State, the Department of the Treasury, Central Intelligence Agency, Interpol and individuals and organizations in the processing of the application or petition for naturalization, or during the course of investigation to elicit further information required by the Immigration and Naturalization Service to carry out its function. Information solicited which indicates a violation or potential violation of law, whether civil, criminal or regulatory in nature may be referred, as routine use, to the appropriate agency, whether federal, state, local or foreign, charged with the responsibility of investigating, enforcing or prosecuting such violations. Failure to provide any or all of the solicited information may result in an adverse recommendation to the court as to an alien's eligibility for naturalization and denial by the court of a petition for naturalization.

For sale by the Superintendent of Documents, U.S. Government Printing Office
Washington, D.C. 20402 (per 100)

U.S. GOVERNMENT PRINTING OFFICE 1980 520-933

N-400   Page 4

UNITED STATES DEPARTMENT OF JUSTICE
IMMIGRATION AND NATURALIZATION SERVICE

Form approved.
OMB No. 43–R0081.

APPLICATION TO FILE PETITION FOR NATURALIZATION IN BEHALF OF CHILD
Under Section 322 of the Immigration and Nationality Act

Take or Mail to:
IMMIGRATION AND NATURALIZATION SERVICE,

CHILD's NAME AND ALIEN REGISTRATION NUMBER

Name ....

No. ....

Date ...., 19.......

I (We), the undersigned, desire that a petition for naturalization be filed in behalf of my (our) child.

(1) My full, true, and correct name is ....
(Full, true name of citizen parent or citizen adoptive parent, without abbreviations)

(2) My present place of residence is ....
(Apt. No.)   (Number and street)   (City or town)   (County)   (State)   (ZIP Code)

(3) I am a citizen of the United States of America and was born on .... in ....
(Month) (Day) (Year)   (City, State, and Country)

(If not a native-born citizen) I was naturalized on .... at ....
(Month) (Day) (Year)   (City and State)

certificate No. ...., or I became a citizen of the United States through ....

(Is the child's other parent a citizen of the United States?   ☐ Yes   ☐ No)
(Complete (1a) to (3a) only if second parent wishes to join in application)

(1a) My full, true, and correct name is ....
(Full, true name of second citizen parent or citizen adoptive parent, without abbreviations)

(2a) My present place of residence is ....
(Apt. No.)   (Number and street)   (City or town)   (County)   (State)   (ZIP Code)

(3a) I am a citizen of the United States of America and was born on .... in ....
(Month) (Day) (Year)   (City, State, and Country)

(If not a native-born citizen) I was naturalized on .... at ....
(Month) (Day) (Year)   (City and State)

certificate No. ...., or I became a citizen of the United States through ....

(4) I am (We are) the parent(s) of ....
(Full, true name of child, without abbreviations)
in whose behalf this application for naturalization is filed.

(5) The said child now resides with me (us) at ....
(Apt. No.)   (Number and street)   (City or town)

...., is ...., and is a citizen, subject, or national of ....
(County)   (State)   (ZIP Code)   (Married) (Single)

(6) The said child was born on .... in ....
(Month) (Day) (Year)   (City and Country)

(7) The said child was lawfully admitted to the United States for permanent residence on .... at
(Month) (Day) (Year)

.... under the name of ....
(City)   (State)

.... and does .... intend to reside permanently in the United States.

(8) I (We) desire the naturalization court to change the name of the child to ....
(Give full name desired, without abbreviations)

(9) If application is in behalf of an adopted child:
I (We) adopted said child on .... in the ....
(Month) (Day) (Year)   (Name of court)

.... at .... before the child was 16 years of age.
(City or town) (State) (Country)

The said child has resided continuously in the United States with me (us) in my (our) legal custody since ....
(Month) (Day) (Year)

N-402   Application to File Petition for Naturalization in Behalf of Child

204

(10) Since such child's lawful admission to the United States for permanent residence, the child has not been absent from the United States at any time except as follows (if none, state "None"):

DEPARTED FROM THE UNITED STATES		RETURNED TO THE UNITED STATES	
PORT	DATE (MONTH, DAY, YEAR)	PORT	DATE (MONTH, DAY, YEAR)

(11) Has such child ever been a patient in a mental institution, or ever been treated for a mental illness? ☐ Yes ☐ No

(12) The law provides that a person may not be regarded as qualified for naturalization under certain conditions, if the person knowingly committed certain offenses or crimes, even though not arrested therefor. Has such child ever in or outside the United States:

    (a) Knowingly committed any crime for which he/she has not been arrested? . . . . ☐ Yes ☐ No

    (b) Been arrested, charged with violation of any law or ordinance, summoned into court as a defendant, convicted, fined, imprisoned, or placed on probation or parole, or forfeited collateral for any act involving a crime, misdemeanor, or breach of any law or ordinance? . . . . ☐ Yes ☐ No

If the answer to (a) or (b) is "Yes," on a separate sheet, give the following information as to each incident: when and where occurred, offense involved, and outcome of case if any.

(13) Are deportation proceedings pending against such child or has such child ever been deported or ordered deported, or has such child ever applied for suspension of deportation or for preexamination? . . . . . . ☐ Yes ☐ No

(14) List the child's membership in every organization, association, fund, foundation, party, club, society, or similar group in the United States and in any other place, during the past ten years, and his foreign military service. (If none, write "None.")

(a) .... , 19 .... to 19 ....

(b) .... , 19 .... to 19 ....

(c) .... , 19 .... to 19 ....

(d) .... , 19 .... to 19 ....

(15) Has such child ever served in the Armed Forces of the United States? . . . . ☐ Yes ☐ No

(16) (Answer only if the child is of an understanding age.) If the law requires it, is the child willing to bear arms or perform noncombatant service in the Armed Forces of the United States or perform work of national importance under civilian direction? If "No" explain fully on a separate sheet of paper . . . . ☐ Yes ☐ No

(17) Since the child's lawful admission to the United States for permanent residence, my wife (husband) and I have been absent from the United States as follows (if no absences, state "None"):

....

....

....

(18) My wife (husband) and I have been married as follows (give information as to each marriage): (Use extra sheet of paper if necessary.)

DATE MARRIED	DATE MARRIAGE ENDED	NAME OF SPOUSE	HOW MARRIAGE ENDED (Death or divorce)

(2)

N-402   Page 2

(19) A petition for naturalization has .... previously been filed on behalf of said child on ....
(not)   (Month) (Day) (Year)

at ....in .... and denied.
(City) (County) (State)   (Name of court)

_____   _____
(Signature of 1st parent)   (Signature of 2d parent)

_____   _____
(Address of 1st parent)   (Address of 2d parent)

_____   _____
(Telephone No.)   (Date)   (Telephone No.)   (Date)

SIGNATURE OF PERSON PREPARING FORM, IF OTHER THAN APPLICANT(S)

I declare that this document was prepared by me at the request of the applicant(s) and is based on all information of which I have any knowledge.

_____   _____   _____
(Signature)   (Address)   (Date)

TO APPLICANTS: DO NOT WRITE BELOW THESE LINES

AFFIDAVIT

· I do swear (affirm) that I know the contents of this application comprising pages 1 to 3, inclusive, subscribed by me; that the same are true to the best of my knowledge and belief; that corrections number ( ) to ( ) were made by me or at my request; and that this application was signed by me with my full, true name.

_____
(Complete and true signature of 1st parent)

_____
(Complete and true signature of 2d parent)

Subscribed and sworn (affirmed) to before me at the preliminary investigation (examination) at .... this .... day of ...., 19......

I certify that before verification the parent(s) stated in my presence that he (she they) had .... read the (heard) foregoing application and corrections therein and understood the contents thereof.

_____
(Naturalization Examiner)

(1st witness. Occupation) ....   Nonfiled ....
(2nd witness. Occupation) ....
                                             (Date, Reasons)

(3)   U.S. GOVERNMENT PRINTING OFFICE : 1980 O—324-396

N-402   Page 3

UNITED STATES DEPARTMENT OF JUSTICE
Immigration and Naturalization Service

Form approved.
OMB No. 43–R0098

APPLICATION TO PRESERVE RESIDENCE FOR NATURALIZATION PURPOSES

(Under Section 316(b) or 317, Immigration and Nationality Act)

(*Please read instructions on reverse*)

Take or mail to:

IMMIGRATION AND NATURALIZATION SERVICE

Fee Stamp

Alien Registration No.

Date of Birth   Place of Birth

1. My full true name is ....

2. My home address in the United States is ....
....
    (City or town)   (Number and street)   (State)

My foreign address (☐ is ☐ will be) ....
    (Zip code)
....
    (City or town)   (Number and street)   (State)

3. I am an alien. I was lawfully admitted to the United States for permanent residence at ....
....   under the name of ....
    (Port of entry)

on ....   on the vessel ....
    (Month)   (Day)   (Year)   (If otherwise than vessel show manner of arrival)

I have resided in and have been physically present in the United States for an uninterrupted period of at least .... year(s) since such lawful entry. Since the date of my lawful entry. I have been absent from the United States as follows (include date of last departure if now abroad, and if necessary attach an additional sheet to show all absences):

Date of departure	Date and port of return	Name of vessel	Purpose of trip

4. Since becoming a permanent resident, have you ever filed an income tax return as a nonresident alien or otherwise claimed or received benefits as a nonresident alien under the income tax laws? ☐ Yes ☐ No

5. I (☐ am, ☐ will be, ☐ was) employed as, or under contract as, ...

by ....
    (Name of employer)

address ....
    (Number and street)   (City or town)   (State)   (Zip code)

Such employment of contract { necessitates / will necessitate / necessitated } my presence in ....
    (Country or countries)

from ....   to ....
    (Month)   (Day)   (Year)   (Month)   (Day)   (Year)

6. My absence from the United States for such periods (☐ is, ☐ will be, ☐ was):
    ☐ on behalf of the United States Government.
    ☐ for the purpose of carrying on scientific research on behalf of an American institution of research.
    ☐ for the purpose of engaging in the development of foreign trade and commerce of the United States on behalf of an American firm or corporation or a subsidiary thereof engaged in the development of such trade and commerce.
    ☐ necessary to the protection of the property rights abroad of an American firm or corporation engaged in the development of foreign trade and commerce of the United States.
    ☐ on behalf of a public international organization of which the United States is a member, by which I was first employed on ...., 19......
    ☐ solely in my capacity as a ☐ clergyman, ☐ missionary, ☐ brother, ☐ nun, or ☐ sister.

7. In support of the foregoing statement of facts I submit the following documents ....
    (See Instructions)

8. I respectfully request that you find my absence under the above-stated conditions to be in compliance with the provisions of Sec. 316(b) or 317 of the Immigration and Nationality Act.

Signature of Person Preparing Form, If Other Than Applicant	Signature of Applicant
I declare that this document was prepared by me at the request of the applicant and is based on all information of which I have any knowledge.	I certify that the above statements are true and correct to the best of my knowledge and belief.
SIGNATURE	COMPLETE SIGNATURE OF APPLICANT
ADDRESS DATE	MAILING ADDRESS: Number, street, city, State, and ZIP code DATE

Form N–470 (Rev. 9–27–75) N

N-470   Application to Preserve Residence for Naturalization Purposes

EXAMINER'S REPORT

I have investigated this application for benefits under Section [(316(b)) (317)] of the Immigration and Nationality Act and find that:

1. The applicant (was) (was not) lawfully admitted for permanent residence, his status (having) (not having) changed.

2. ☐ Applicant for benefits of Section 316(b):
   (a) (Has) (Has not) resided in and been physically present in the United States for an uninterrupted period of at least one year after lawful admission for permanent residence.
   (b) (Has) (Has not) filed the application before being absent from the United States for a continuous period of one year.
   (c) [(Is) (Is not) (Will be) (Will not be)] employed or under contract as alleged in this application; and the employer or contractor named in this application (is) (is not) engaged in the type of business described in Section 316(b).

3. ☐ Applicant for the benefits of Section 317:
   (a) (Has) (Has not) been physically present and residing in the United States for an uninterrupted period of at least one year after lawful admission for permanent residence.
   (b) [(Is) (Is not) (Will be) (Will not be) (Was) (Was not)] absent solely for the purpose alleged in this application; and the denomination or organization named in this application (is) (is not) of the class described in Section 317.

4. Supplemental report or order (is) (is not) attached.

5. I recommend that the application be (granted) (denied).

....
(Signature of Examiner)

....
(Title)   (Date)

ORDER

It is Ordered that the within-named applicant be .... granted the benefits applied for in this application to cover absence from the United States from the date stated therein to an indefinite date thereafter so long as (s)he remains in the employment and is absent for the purposes alleged therein.

....
(District Director)

....
(Date)

U.S. GOVERNMENT PRINTING OFFICE : 1975—O— 863 478

GPO 964-011

N-470   Page 2

UNITED STATES DEPARTMENT OF JUSTICE
Immigration and Naturalization Service

Form Approved
OMB No. 43-R0099

Alien Registration
No. _____

APPLICATION FOR A NEW NATURALIZATION OR CITIZENSHIP PAPER

Fee Stamp

Take or mail to
IMMIGRATION AND NATURALIZATION SERVICE,

I hereby apply for a new: ☐ Certificate of Citizenship ☐ Certificate of Naturalization ☐ Certificate of Repatriation ☐ Declaration of Intention.

(1)(a) My full, true name is _____
(b) The name in which my paper was issued was _____
(c) Other names I have used are _____
(2) I now reside at _____
(3) I was born at _____
    (Apt. No.)   (Number and street)   (City or town)   (County)   (State)   (Zip Code)
    (City or town)   (Country)   on   (Month)   (Day)   (Year)
(4) I arrived in the United States at _____
    (City or town)   (State)   on   (Month)   (Day)   (Year)
(5a) My personal description is: Sex _____; complexion _____; color of eyes _____;
color of hair _____; height _____ feet _____ inches; weight _____ pounds; visible distinctive
marks _____ marital status _____;
(5b) Country of which I was a citizen, subject, or national _____
(6) The naturalization or citizenship paper was issued to me by _____
    ("Immigration & Naturalization Service" or name of court)
at _____
    (City or town)   (County)   (State)   on   (Month)   (Day)   (Year)
(7) (If applicable) Since becoming a citizen, I ☐ have ☐ have not lost my citizenship in any manner.
(8) Since the date the naturalization or citizenship paper was issued to me I have not been absent from the United States for more than six months, except as follows: (If none, state "none.")

DEPARTED FROM THE UNITED STATES			RETURNED TO THE UNITED STATES		
Port	Date (Month, Day, Year)	Vessel, or Other Means of Conveyance	Port	Date (Month, Day, Year)	Vessel, or Other Means of Conveyance

(9) (If applicable) Such paper became ☐ Lost ☐ Mutilated ☐ Destroyed on or about _____
    (Month)   (Day)   (Year)
at _____
    (City or town)   (State or country)   under the following circumstances: _____

In addition to the above, answer Number 10 if you are applying for a new certificate in a changed name.

(10) My name was changed to my present name by —
(a) Marriage at _____
    (City or town)   (County)   (State)   on   (Date)
(b) Decree of _____ Court, at _____
    (City or town)
    (County)   (State)   on   (Month)   (Day)   (Year)

Signature of person preparing form, if other than applicant

Signature of Applicant

I declare that this document was prepared by me at the request of the applicant and is based on all information of which I have any knowledge.
Signature:

Address   Date

Mailing Address: Number, Street, City, State, and Zip Code

Telephone Number

Form N-565 (Rev.11-26-79)N

N-565   Application for a New Naturalization or Citizenship Paper

209

AFFIDAVIT

I do swear that I know the content of this application signed by me; that the same are true to the best of my knowledge and belief; and that corrections numbered ( ) to ( ) were made by me or at my request. _____

(Signature of applicant)

Subscribed and sworn to before me by the applicant at _____ this
_____ day of _____ 19__. _____

(Officer's signature and title)

EXAMINER'S REPORT

I have investigated this application and I am satisfied that the applicant is _____ the person to whom the original record relates and that the applicant has _____ become expatriated subsequent to acquiring United States citizenship, and that the naturalization or citizenship paper described in the application has _____ been _____

_____
(Lost, mutilated, destroyed, surrendered)

The naturalization or declaration has _____ been verified.

Supplemental report is _____ attached hereto.

I recommend that the application be _____ granted.

_____
(Signature)

Approved: _____ _____ , 19 ___ _____
(Title of officer making report)

_____
(District Director)

_____
(Date)   (Applicant's signature)

GPO 964-608

N-565   Page 2

UNITED STATES DEPARTMENT OF JUSTICE
IMMIGRATION AND NATURALIZATION SERVICE

APPLICATION FOR CERTIFICATE
OF CITIZENSHIP

FEE STAMP

Form approved.
OMB No. 043 R0105.

Take or mail this application to:
IMMIGRATION AND NATURALIZATION SERVICE

(Print or type) .... nee ....
(Full, True Name, without Abbreviations)   (Maiden name, if any)

Date ....

....
(Apartment number, Street address, and, if appropriate, "in care of")

....
(City)   (County)   (State)   (ZIP Code)

ALIEN REGISTRATION
No. ....

....
(Telephone Number)

(SEE INSTRUCTIONS. BE SURE YOU UNDERSTAND EACH QUESTION BEFORE YOU ANSWER IT.)
I hereby apply to the Commissioner of Immigration and Naturalization for a certificate showing that I am a citizen of the United States of America.

(1) I was born in .... on ....
(City)   (State or country)   (Month) (Day) (Year)

(2) My personal description is: Sex ....; complexion ....; color of eyes ....; color of hair ....;
height .... feet .... inches; weight .... pounds; visible distinctive marks ....
.... Marital status: ☐ Single;   ☐ Married;   ☐ Divorced;   ☐ Widow(er).

(3) I arrived in the United States at .... on ....
(City and State)   (Month) (Day) (Year)
under the name .... by means of ....
(Name of ship or other means of arrival)
☐ on U.S. Passport No. .... issued to me at .... on ....
☐ on an Immigrant Visa.   ☐ Other (specify) ....   (Month) (Day) (Year)

(4) **FILL IN THIS BLOCK ONLY IF YOU ARRIVED IN THE UNITED STATES BEFORE JULY 1, 1924.**
(a) My last permanent foreign residence was ....
(City)   (Country)
(b) I took the ship or other conveyance to the United States at ....
(City)   (Country)
(c) I was coming to .... at ....
(Name of person in the United States)   (City and State where this person was living)
(d) I traveled to the United States with ....
(Names of passengers or relatives with whom you traveled, and their relationship to you, if any)

(5) Have you been out of the United States since you first arrived? ☐ Yes ☐ No. If "Yes" fill in the following information for every absence.

DATE DEPARTED	DATE RETURNED	NAME OF AIRLINE, OR OTHER MEANS USED TO RETURN TO THE UNITED STATES	PORT OF RETURN TO THE UNITED STATES

(6) I (have) (have not) filed a petition for naturalization.

(If "have", attach full explanation.)
TO THE APPLICANT.—Do not write between the double lines below. Continue on next page.

ARRIVAL RECORDS EXAMINED
Card index ....
Index books ....
Manifests ....
....
....
....

ARRIVAL RECORD FOUND
Place .... Date ....
Name ....
Manner ....
Marital status .... Age ....
(Signature of person making search)

Form N-600 (Rev. 11-26-79)N   (1)

N-600   Application for Certificate of Citizenship

(CONTINUE HERE)

(7) I claim United States citizenship through my *(check whichever applicable)* ☐ father; ☐ mother; ☐ both parents;

☐ adoptive parent(s)   ☐ husband

(8) My father's name is ....; he was born on ....
$\qquad$ (Month)   (Day)   (Year)

at ....; and resides at ....
$\qquad$ (City) $\qquad$ (State or country) $\qquad$ (Street address, city, and State or country. If dead, write

.... He became a citizen of the United States by ☐ birth; ☐ naturalization on ....
"dead" and date of death.) $\qquad$ (Month)   (Day)   (Year)

in the .... Certificate of Naturalization No. ....;
$\qquad$ (Name of court, city, and State)

☐ through his parent(s), and ...... (was)   (was not) ...... issued Certificate of Citizenship No. A or AA ....

(If known) His former Alien Registration No. was ....

He (has) (has not) lost United States citizenship. *(If citizenship lost, attach full explanation.)*

He resided in the United States from .... to ....; from .... to ....; from .... to ....;
$\qquad$ (Year) $\qquad$ (Year) $\qquad$ (Year) $\qquad$ (Year) $\qquad$ (Year) $\qquad$ (Year)

from .... to ....; from .... to ....; I am the child of his .... marriage.
$\qquad$ (Year) $\qquad$ (Year) $\qquad$ (Year) $\qquad$ (Year) $\qquad$ (1st, 2d, 3d, etc.)

(9) My mother's present name is ....; her maiden name was ....;

she was born on ....; at ....; she resides
$\qquad$ (Month)   (Day)   (Year) $\qquad$ (City) $\qquad$ (State or country)

at .... She became a citizen of the United States
$\qquad$ (Street address, city, and State or country. If dead, write "dead" and date of death.)

by ☐ birth; ☐ naturalization under the name of ....

on ....; in the ....;
$\qquad$ (Month)   (Day)   (Year) $\qquad$ (Name of court, city, and State)

Certificate of Naturalization No. ....; ☐ through her parent(s), and ...... (was)   (was not) ...... issued Certificate

of Citizenship No. A or AA .... (If known) Her former Alien Registration No. was ....

She (has) (has not) lost United States citizenship. *(If citizenship lost, attach full explanation.)*

She resided in the United States from .... to ....; from .... to ....; from .... to ....; from ....
$\qquad$ (Year) $\qquad$ (Year) $\qquad$ (Year) $\qquad$ (Year) $\qquad$ (Year) $\qquad$ (Year) $\qquad$ (Year)

to ....; from .... to ....; I am the child of her .... marriage.
$\qquad$ (Year) $\qquad$ (Year) $\qquad$ (Year) $\qquad$ (1st, 2d, 3d, etc.)

(10) My mother and my father were married to each other on .... at ....
$\qquad$ (Month)   (Day)   (Year) $\qquad$ (City) $\qquad$ (State or country)

(11) If claim is through adoptive parent(s):

I was adopted on ....; in the ....
$\qquad$ (Month)   (Day)   (Year) $\qquad$ (Name of Court)

at .... before I was 16 years of age by my ....
$\qquad$ (City or town)   (State)   (Country) $\qquad$ (mother, father, parents)

(12) My (father)   (mother) served in the Armed Forces of the United States from ....
$\qquad$ (Date)

to .... and ..(was)   (was not).. honorably discharged.
$\qquad$ (Date)

(13) I (have) (have not) lost my United States citizenship. *(If citizenship lost, attach full explanation.)*

(14) I submit the following documents with this application:

Nature of Document	Names of Persons Concerned
....	....
....	....
....	....
....	....
....	....

(2)

N-600   Page 2

(15) Fill in this block if your brother, sister, mother or father ever applied to the Immigration Service for a certificate of citizenship.

Name of Relative	Relationship	Date of Birth	When Application Submitted	Certificate No. and File No., If Known, and Location of Office

(16) Fill in this block only if you are now or ever have been a married woman. I have been married .... time(s), as follows:

Date Married	Name of Husband	Citizenship of Husband	If Marriage Has Been Terminated: Date Marriage Ended	How Marriage Ended (Death or divorce)

(17) Fill in this block only if you claim citizenship through a husband. (*Marriage must have occurred prior to September 22, 1922.*)
Name of citizen husband .... (Give full and complete name); he was born on ...... (Month) (Day) (Year)
at .... (City) .... (State or country); and resides at .... (Street address, city, and State or country. If dead, write "dead" and date of death.)
He became a citizen of the United States by ☐ birth; ☐ naturalization on ...... (Month) (Day) (Year)
in the .... (Name of court, city, and State) .... Certificate of Naturalization No. ....;
☐ through his parent(s), and (was) (was not) issued Certificate of Citizenship No. A or AA ....
He (has) (has not) since lost United States citizenship. (*If citizenship lost, attach full explanation.*)
I am of the .... race. Before my marriage to him, he was married .... time(s), as follows: (1, 2, 3, etc.)

Date Married	Name of Wife	If Marriage Has Been Terminated: Date Marriage Ended	How Marriage Ended (Death or divorce)

(18) Fill in this block only if you claim citizenship through your stepfather. (*Applicable only if mother married U.S. Citizen prior to September 22, 1922.*)
The full name of my stepfather is .... ; he was born on ...... (Month) (Day) (Year)
at .... (City) .... (State or country); and resides at .... (Street address, city, and State or country. If dead, write "dead" and date of death.)
He became a citizen of the United States by ☐ birth; ☐ naturalization on ...... (Month) (Day) (Year)
in the .... (Name of court, city, and State) .... Certificate of Naturalization No. ....;
☐ through his parent(s), and (was) (was not) issued Certificate of Citizenship No. A or AA ....
He (has) (has not) since lost United States citizenship. (*If citizenship lost, attach full explanation.*)
He and my mother were married to each other on .... (Month) (Day) (Year) at .... (City and State or country)
My mother is of the .... race. She (was) (was not) issued Certificate of Citizenship No. A ....
Before marrying my mother, my stepfather was married .... time(s), as follows: (1, 2, 3, etc.)

Date Married	Name of Wife	If Marriage Has Been Terminated: Date Marriage Ended	How Marriage Ended (Death or divorce)

(19) I (have) (have not) previously applied for a certificate of citizenship on .... (Date), at .... (Office)

(20) Signature of person preparing form, if other than applicant. I declare that this document was prepared by me at the request of the applicant and is based on all information of which I have any knowledge.
SIGNATURE: ....
ADDRESS: .... DATE: ....

(SIGN HERE) .... (Signature of applicant or parent or guardian)

(3)

AFFIDAVIT

I, the ...., do swear
(Applicant, parent, guardian)
that I know and understand the contents of this application,
signed by me, and of attached supplementary pages numbered ( ) to ( ), inclusive; that the same are true to the
best of my knowledge and belief; and that corrections numbered ( ) to ( ) were made by me or at my request.

Subscribed and sworn to before me upon examination of the
applicant (parent, guardian) at ....
....................., this .... day of ...., 19......
and continued solely for:

....
(Signature of applicant, parent, guardian)

....
(Officer's Signature and Title)

REPORT AND RECOMMENDATION ON APPLICATION

On the basis of the documents, records, and persons examined, and the identification upon personal appearance of the underage
beneficiary, I find that all the facts and conclusions set forth under oath in this application are .... true and correct; that the
applicant did .... derive or acquire United States citizenship on ...., through
(Month) (Day) (Year)

and that (s)he _(has)_ _(has not)_ been expatriated since that time. I recommend that this application be (granted) (denied) and that
_(A)_ _(AA)_ Certificate of citizenship be .... issued in the name of --
In addition to the documents listed in Item 14, the following documents and records have been examined:

Person Examined	Address	Relationship to Applicant	Date Testimony Heard
....	....	....	....
	....	....	....
....	....		

Supplementary Report(s) No.(s) .... Attached.
Date ----------------------, 19-----.

(Officer's Signature and Title)

I do .... concur in the recommendation.

Date ...., 19.....

....
(Signature of District Director or Officer in Charge)

(4)

N-600   Page 4

214

List of Offices of the Immigration and Naturalization Service from Which Further Information and Forms May Be Obtained

Agana, GU 96910
801 Pacific News
Bldg. P.O. Box DX

Albany, NY 12207
Room 220 U.S. Post
Office and Court-
house
445 Broadway

*Anchorage, AK
99513
Federal Bldg., U.S.
Courthouse
701 "C" St., Rm. D
229

*Atlanta, GA 30303
Rm. 1408 Richard B.
Russell Fed. Office
Bldg.
75 Spring St. S.W.

*Baltimore, MD
21201
E. A. Garmatz Fed-
eral Bldg.
100 South Hanover
Street

*Boston, MA 02203
John Fitzgerald Ken-
nedy Federal Bldg.
Government
Center

*Buffalo, NY 14202
68 Court Street

Charlotte, NC 28231
Charles R. Jonas Fed-
eral Bldg.
401 W. Trade St.,
P.O. Box 31247

*Chicago, IL 60604
Dirksen Federal Of-
fice Bldg.
219 South Dearborn
St.

Cincinnati, OH
45201
U.S. Post Office &
Courthouse
5th and Walnut Sts.
P.O. Box 537

*Cleveland, OH
44199
Anthony J. Cele-
brezze Federal
Building
1240 East 9th Street,
Room 1917

*Dallas, TX 75242
Room 6A21, Federal
Building
1100 Commerce St.

*Denver, CO 80202
17027 Federal Office
Bldg.

*Detroit, MI 48207
Federal Building
333 Mt. Elliott Street

*El Paso, TX 79984
343 U.S. Court-
house
P.O. Box 9398

Fresno, CA 93721
Federal Bldg., U.S.
Courthouse
1130 "O" St.

Hammond, IN
46320
104 Federal Building
507 State Street

*Harlingen, TX 78550
719 Grimes Avenue

*Hartford, CT 06105
900 Asylum Ave.

*Helena, MT 59601
Federal Building
301 South Park
Room 512

*Honolulu, HI 96809
595 Ala
Moana
Boulevard
P.O. Box 461

*Houston, TX 77208
Federal Building
515 Rusk Avenue
P.O. Box 61630

*Jacksonville, FL
32201
Rm. 227 Post Office
Building
311 W. Monroe St.,
P.O. Box 4608

*Kansas City, MO
64106
Suite 1100
324 E. Eleventh St.

Las Vegas, NV
89101
Federal Building,
U.S. Courthouse
300 Las Vegas Blvd.,
South

*Los Angeles, CA
90012
300 North Los Ange-
les Street

Memphis, TN 38103
814 Federal Bldg.
167 North Main St.

*Miami, FL 33130
Room 1324, Federal
Building
51 S.W. First Avenue

Milwaukee, WI
53202
Rm. 186, Federal
Building
517 East Wisconsin
Avenue

*Newark, NJ 07102
Federal Building
970 Broad Street

*New Orleans, LA
70113
Postal Service Build-
ing
701 Loyola Avenue

*New York, NY
10007
26 Federal Plaza

Norfolk, VA 23510
Norfolk Federal Bldg.
200 Granby Mall,
Rm. 439

*Omaha, NE 68102
Room 1008, New
Federal Bldg.
106 South 15th Street

*Philadelphia, PA
19106
Room 1321, U.S.
Courthouse
Independence
Mall West
601 Market Street

*Phoenix, AZ 85025
Federal Bldg.
230 North First Ave-
nue

Pittsburgh, PA 15222
2130 Federal Build-
ing
1000 Liberty Avenue

*Portland, ME 04112
76 Pearl St.

*Portland, OR 97209
Federal Office Build-
ing
511 NW Broad-
way

Providence, RI
02903
Federal Building,
U.S. Post Office
Exchange Terrace

Reno, NV 89502
Suite 150
350 South Center
Street

Sacramento, CA
95814
Federal & U.S. Court-
house Bldg.
Rm. 1-060
630 Capitol Mall

*St. Albans, VT 05478
Federal Building
P.O. Box 591

St. Louis, MO 63101
Room 423, U.S.
Courthouse and
Customhouse
1114 Market Street

*INDICATES DISTRICT OFFICE

*St. Paul, MN 55101
927 Main Post Office
Bldg.
180 E. Kellogg Blvd.

Salt Lake City, UT
84138
Room 4103
New Federal Build-
ing
125 South State
Street

*San Antonio, TX
78206
U.S. Federal Building
727 East Durango
Suite A301

*San Diego, CA
92188
880 Front St.

*San Francisco, CA
94111
Appraisers Bldg.
630 Sansome Street

*San Juan, PR 00936
GPO Box 5068

Santa Ana, CA
92701
701 W. 17th St.

*Seattle, WA 98134
815 Airport Way,
South

Spokane, WA 99201
691 U.S. Court-
house Building

Tampa, FL 33602
Rm. 539, 500 Zack
St.

*Washington, DC
20538
25 E St., NW.

The Whipple 'Peace Flag' of forty-eight stars, designed by Wayne Whipple in 1912, was chosen the winner out of five hundred competitors, and approved by President William Howard Taft. The design recalls the succession of American statehood, with a "great star" of thirteen stars at center, surrounded by two rings of stars — the inner one with twenty-five stars for the number of additional states until the First Centennial, and the outer ring representing the states admitted to the Union since 1877.

Citizenship

(Questions 1-15)

Questions 1-10

Put an "X" in the box under TRUE if the statement is CORRECT. Put an "X" in the box under FALSE is the statement is INCORRECT.

	TRUE	FALSE
1. Legally admitted immigrants are required to become American citizens.	☐	☐
2. There are more than 225 million people living in the United States.	☐	☐
3. Persons of any race can become naturalized citizens of the United States.	☐	☐
4. Most people living in the United States are native-born Americans.	☐	☐
5. In a democracy such as ours, political and social changes are achieved through legislation.	☐	☐
6. All American citizens have the right to vote.	☐	☐
7. Voting in the United States is by secret ballot.	☐	☐
8. Electioneering is permitted at the polling places.	☐	☐
9. Voters are required to join political parties.	☐	☐
10. Voting is compulsory for all American citizens.	☐	☐

Questions 11-15

Underline the correct word or words in parentheses in each of the following statements:

11. The United States is (almost as large as, as large as, larger than) all of Europe.

12. The United States is the (largest, second largest, fourth largest) country in the world.

13. The legal process by which an alien becomes an American citizen is called (immigration, naturalization, registration).

14. A person who keeps moving from one part of the country to another part in search of work is called (an alien, a migrant, an Indian).

15. The privilege of voting is given to (all, male, qualified) citizens.

American History

(Questions 16-65)

Questions 16-25

Column I lists famous names in American history. Before each name in Column I, place the letter in front of the phrase in Column II for which each is noted.

Column I

16. ___Christopher Columbus

17. ___Jefferson Davis

18. ___Dwight D. Eisenhower

19. ___Thomas Jefferson

20. ___Francis Scott Key

21. ___Abraham Lincoln

22. ___Franklin D. Roosevelt

23. ___George Washington

24. ___Roger Williams

25. ___Woodrow Wilson

Column II

(A) Author of the Declaration of Independence

(B) Confederate president

(C) Discoverer of America

(D) First president of the United States

(E) Founder of Rhode Island

(F) "Four Freedoms"

(G) President of the United States during the Civil War

(H) President of the United States during World War I

(I) "The Star-Spangled Banner"

(J) World War II military leader who later became president

Questions 26-40

Put an "X" in the box under TRUE if the statement is CORRECT. Put an "X" in the box under FALSE if the statement is INCORRECT.

	TRUE	FALSE
26. The Indians inhabited America before the early settlers arrived on this continent.	☐	☐
27. Christopher Columbus was an Italian navigator.	☐	☐
28. John Cabot was the first Englishman to explore America.	☐	☐
29. The first permanent English settlement in America was established at Plymouth.	☐	☐

30. The thirteen states were governed by the Articles of Confederation before the adoption of the Constitution. ☐ ☐

31. Provisions for a strong executive government were contained in the Articles of Confederation. ☐ ☐

32. The colonies received help from France during the War of Independence. ☐ ☐

33. Under the Constitution, the government became a strong and effective union. ☐ ☐

34. The first capital of the United States was located in New York. ☐ ☐

35. The War of 1812 established the principle that no state has the right to secede from the United States. ☐ ☐

36. The Emancipation Proclamation abolished slavery in the United States. ☐ ☐

37. The United States entered World War I in 1914. ☐ ☐

38. The Social Security Act established old-age benefits and unemployment insurance. ☐ ☐

39. V-E day is the day Japan signed the surrender terms. ☐ ☐

40. The United Nations headquarters is located in New York. ☐ ☐

Questions 41-55

Underline the correct word or words in parentheses in each of the following statements:

41. Queen Isabella of Spain financed the explorations of (John Cabot, Christopher Columbus, Amerigo Vespucci).

42. The early settlers were called (colonists, federalists, royalists).

43. The first permanent English settlement in America was named after (King Henry, Queen Isabella, King James).

44. Most of the first immigrants to settle in America came from (England, France, Holland).

45. The Declaration of Independence was adopted in (1773, 1776, 1789).

46. "The United States of America" was first used officially in the (Articles of Confederation, Constitution of the United States, Declaration of Independence).

47. "All men are created equal" is a quotation from the (Constitution of the United States, Declaration of Independence, Magna Charta).

48. "Taxation without representation is tyranny!" was the slogan used during the (Civil War, Revolutionary War, War of 1812).

49. "The Star-Spangled Banner" was written during the (Civil War, Revolutionary War, War of 1812).

50. The Monroe Doctrine was a declaration of (foreign policy, human freedom, religious freedom).

51. Before the Civil War, slavery was concentrated to a large extent in the (North, South, West).

52. The Emancipation Proclamation was issued by (Robert E. Lee, Abraham Lincoln, William T. Sherman).

53. Alaska was purchased from (France, Russia, Spain).

54. The Statue of Liberty was presented to the United States by (England, France, Germany).

55. The famous American military leader who served in the Pacific during World War II was (Douglas MacArthur, George S. Patton, John J. Pershing).

Questions 56-65

Complete each of the following statements:

56. The first plan of democratic government in America, drawn up by the Pilgrims, was called. . . . .

57. The First Continental Congress met in the city of . . . .

58. The American patriot known as the "Father of Our Country" was . . . .

59. The Louisiana Territory was purchased by the United States from . . . .

60. The second war the United States fought with England was called. . . . .

61. Florida was purchased by the United States from . . . .

62. The Gettysburg Address was delivered by President . . . .

63. The only American president to break the two-term tradition was . . . .

64. The name of the international organization established in 1945 is . . . .

65. . . . . is the largest labor union in the United States.

(Questions 66-125)

Questions 66-75

Column I lists terms commonly used in American government. Before each term in Column I, place the letter in front of the word or phrase in Column II which describes it best.

Column I	Column II
66. ___Congressional Record	(A) Eagle
67. ___Democratic party	(B) "Lower House"
68. ___House of Representatives	(C) Official journal
69. ___National anthem	(D) Presiding officer of the Senate
70. ___National capital	(E) Star
71. ___President's residence	(F) System of checks and balances
72. ___Republican party	(G) "The Star-Spangled Banner"
73. ___Senate	(H) "Upper House"
74. ___Separation of powers	(I) Washington, D.C.
75. ___Vice-president	(J) "White House"

Questions 76-95

Put an "X" in the box under TRUE if the statement is CORRECT. Put an "X" in the box under FALSE if the statement is INCORRECT.

	TRUE	FALSE
76. The president and the vice-president are elected directly by the people.	☐	☐
77. The president's term of office is four years.	☐	☐

78. The president of the United States may be elected for more than two consecutive terms. ☐ ☐

79. No American president has ever resigned from office. ☐ ☐

80. The vice-president takes over the office of the presidency in the event the president dies. ☐ ☐

81. Major presidential appointments must be approved by the Senate. ☐ ☐

82. Naturalized citizens can run for any public office. ☐ ☐

83. Voting for candidates from more than one political party is called voting a split ticket. ☐ ☐

84. The attorney general is the head of the Department of Justice. ☐ ☐

85. Visitors are not permitted to watch Congress in session. ☐ ☐

86. Each state has the same number of representatives. ☐ ☐

87. Each state has the same number of senators. ☐ ☐

88. The Senate must originate all revenue bills. ☐ ☐

89. The right to declare war rests with Congress. ☐ ☐

90. Supreme Court justices are appointed by the president. ☐ ☐

91. The Supreme Court naturalizes aliens. ☐ ☐

92. The federal Supreme Court is the highest court of the land. ☐ ☐

93. The American flag is also called the "Stars and Stripes." ☐ ☐

94. Uncle Sam is the official symbol of the United States. ☐ ☐

95. The national emblem of the United States is the American bald eagle. ☐ ☐

Questions 96-110

Underline the correct word or words in parentheses in each of the following statements:

96. In a democracy, the actual power and authority to rule is held by the (army, people, president).

97. (Great Britain, Holland, The United States) is both a republic and a representative democracy.

98. Most of the federal revenue comes from (customs duties, excise taxes, income taxes).

99. A person must be at least (25, 35, 45) years old to be elected president of the United States.

100. Members of the president's Cabinet are (appointed by the president, elected by the people, selected by Congress).

101. There are (11, 12, 13) executive departments in the national government.

102. The (Commission on Human Rights, Government Printing Office, Library of Congress) is an independent agency in the executive branch.

103. The General Accounting Office is directly responsible to (Congress, the president, the Supreme Court).

104. Congress (carries out, interprets, makes) the laws.

105. Members of the House of Representatives are elected for (2, 4, 6) years.

106. Senators are elected for (2, 4, 6) years.

107. A person must be at least (25, 30, 35) years old to be elected to the United States Senate.

108. Treaties made with foreign countries must be ratified by the (House of Representatives, Senate, Supreme Court).

109. Justices of the United States Supreme Court are appointed for (4 years, 10 years, life).

110. The Supreme Court can be abolished only by (act of Congress, constitutional amendment, executive order).

Questions 111-125

Complete each of the following statements:

111. The colors of the flag of the United States are . . . .

112. The. . . . . hangs in Independence Hall at Philadelphia.

113. Both sides of the Great Seal appear on the reverse side of every . . . . bill.

114. The two major political parties in the United States are the. and the . . . .

115. The power of the President to disapprove a bill passed by both houses of Congress is called the ....

116. The executive department whose chief functions are concerned with foreign affairs is ....

117. The executive department whose chief functions are concerned with managing the nation's financial affairs is ....

118. The name of the most recently established executive department is ....

119. In the event that both the president and the vice-president are unable to perform their duties, the................................ is next in the order of succession.

120. The Senate consists of .... members.

121. There are........................ justices on the Supreme Court.

122. The oath taken by the president at the inauguration is generally administered by the ....

123. Influencing legislators to vote for or against proposed legislation is called...

124. Delaying tactics used by lawmakers to prevent action on matters being considered by the legislators is termed...................

125. To.......................................means to charge a public official with misconduct while in office.

The Constitution of the United States
(Questions 126-155)

Questions 126-135

Put an "X" in the box under TRUE if the statement is CORRECT. Put an "X" in the box under FALSE if the statement is INCORRECT.

TRUE   FALSE

126. The Articles of Confederation was the plan of government prior to the adoption of the Constitution.   ☐   ☐

127. Government under the Articles of Confederation was satisfactory.   ☐   ☐

128. Under the Articles of Confederation, each state retained its full independence.   ☐   ☐

129. No individual rights were included in the Constitution before the Bill of Rights was adopted. ☐ ☐

130. The major objection to the ratification of the Constitution was that it did not guarantee individual liberty. ☐ ☐

131. Those who opposed ratification of the Constitution were called Federalists. ☐ ☐

132. The rights and freedoms guaranteed by the Bill of Rights are for citizens only. ☐ ☐

133. Due process of law is one of the rights guaranteed by the Bill of Rights. ☐ ☐

134. The right to vote regardless of race, color or previous condition of servitude is guaranteed by the Bill of Rights. ☐ ☐

135. A proposed constitutional amendment is not submitted to the president for his approval. ☐ ☐

Questions 136-140

Underline the correct word or words in parentheses in each of the following statements:

136. "We, the people . . ." is a quotation from the (Amendments to the Constitution, First Article of the Constitution, Preamble to the Constitution).

137. The Bill of Rights protects the people against (high taxes, jury duty, religious persecution).

138. The Constitution provides that a national census be taken every (5, 10, 20) years.

139. The Constitution may be changed by (act of Congress, constitutional amendment, executive order).

140. The 19th Amendment gave (aliens, Negroes, women) the right to vote.

Questions 141-145

Complete each of the following statements:

141. The first 10 amendments to the Constitution are called . . . .
. . . .

142. The only amendment ever to be repealed was the . . . .
Amendment.

143. Women could not vote in the United States before the year . . . .

144. The. . . . . Amendment is known as the "Lame Duck" Amendment.

145. There are. amendments to the Constitution.

Questions 146-155

Column I lists several important amendments to the Constitution. Before each amendment in Column I, place the letter in front of the phrase in Column II which describes it.

Column I	Column II
146. ____10th Amendment	(A) Income tax
147. ____13th Amendment	(B) National prohibition
148. ____15th Amendment	(C) Negro suffrage
149. ____16th Amendment	(D) Popular election of senators
150. ____17th Amendment	(E) Presidential disability and succession
151. ____18th Amendment	(F) Presidential electors for District of Columbia
152. ____21st Amendment	(G) Repeal of prohibition
153. ____22nd Amendment	(H) Rights reserved to the states
154. ____23rd Amendment	(I) Slavery abolished
155. ____25th Amendment	(J) Two-term limitation for the presidency

State and Local Government

(Questions 156-175)

Questions 156-160

Put an "X" in the box under TRUE if the statement is CORRECT. Put an "X" in the box under FALSE if the statement is INCORRECT.

TRUE   FALSE

156. The term of office for governor varies in different states.   ☐   ☐

157. All state legislatures consist of two houses.   ☐   ☐

158. There are 50 states in the United States. □ □

159. States cannot impose tariffs on imports from other countries. □ □

160. Each city has its own constitution. □ □

Questions 161-165

Underline the correct word or words in parentheses in each of the following statements:

161. The (governor, mayor, president) is the chief executive of the state.

162. State constitutions are not higher than (local ordinances, state laws, the federal Constitution).

163. Governors are (appointed by the president, elected by the people of their states, selected by the state legislatures).

164. (Alaska, California, Texas) is the largest state in the United States.

165. Alaska was the (48th, 49th, 50th) state to be admitted into the United States.

Questions 166-175

Complete each of the following statements:

166. If the governor dies, the .... takes over the governorship.

167. Each state, regardless of size, is represented by.................... senators in the United States Congress.

168. States are generally subdivided into ....

169. .... is the smallest state in the United States.

170. .... is the only state that is not located on the North American continent.

171. A new state can be established only by ....

172. A state can be sued by another state in the .... Court.

173. The name of the most recently admitted state is ....

174. Members of the state legislature are elected by ....

175. The state legislative houses are usually called the House of Representatives or the Assembly and the ....

Answers
to Review Questions

Questions 1-10

1. false; 2. true; 3. true; 4. true; 5. true; 6. false; 7. true; 8. false; 9. false; 10. false.

Questions 11-15

11. almost as large as; 12. fourth largest; 13. naturalization; 14. a migrant; 15. qualified.

Questions 16-25

16. C; 17. B; 18. J; 19. A; 20. I; 21. G; 22. F; 23. D; 24. E; 25. H.

Questions 26-40

26. true; 27. true; 28. true; 29. false; 30. true; 31. false; 32. true; 33. true; 34. true; 35. false; 36. false; 37. false; 38. true; 39. false; 40. true.

Questions 41-55

41. Christopher Columbus; 42. colonists; 43. King James; 44. England; 45. 1776; 46. Declaration of Independence; 47. Declaration of Independence; 48. Revolutionary War; 49. War of 1812; 50. foreign policy; 51. South; 52. Abraham Lincoln; 53. Russia; 54. France; 55. Douglas MacArthur.

Questions 56-65

56. the Mayflower Compact; 57. Philadelphia; 58. George Washington; 59. France; 60. the War of 1812; 61. Spain; 62. Lincoln; 63. Franklin D. Roosevelt; 64. the United Nations; 65. the A.F.L.-C.I.O.

Questions 66-75

66. C; 67. E; 68. B; 69. G; 70. I; 71. J; 72. A; 73. H; 74. F; 75. D.

Questions 76-95

76. false; 77. true; 78. false; 79. false; 80. true; 81. true; 82. false;

83. true; 84. true; 85. false; 86. false; 87. true; 88. false; 89. true; 90. true; 91. false; 92. true; 93. true; 94. false; 95. true.

Questions 96-110

96. people; 97. The United States; 98. income taxes; 99. 35; 100. appointed by the president; 101. 13; 102. Commission on Human Rights; 103. Congress; 104. makes; 105. 2; 106. 6; 107. 30; 108. Senate; 109. life; 110. constitutional amendment.

Questions 111-125

111. red, white and blue; 112. Liberty Bell; 113. one-dollar; 114. Democratic party, Republican party; 115. veto; 116. the Department of State; 117. Treasury Department; 118. the Department of Education; 119. Speaker of the House; 120. 100; 121. 9; 122. Chief Justice of the United States; 123. lobbying; 124. fillibuster; 125. impeach.

Questions 126-135

126. true; 127. false; 128. true; 129. false; 130. true; 131. false; 132. false; 133. true; 134. false; 135. true.

Questions 136-140

136. Preamble to the Constitution; 137. religious persecution; 138. 10; 139. constitutional amendment; 140. women.

Questions 141-145

141. the Bill of Rights; 142. 18th; 143. 1920; 144. 20th; 145. 26.

Questions 146-155

146. H; 147. I; 148. C; 149. A; 150. D; 151. B; 152. G; 153. J; 154. F; 155. E.

Questions 156-160

156. true; 157. false; 158. true; 159. true; 160. false.

Questions 161-165

161. governor; 162. the federal Constitution; 163. elected by the people of their states; 164. Alaska; 165. 49th.

Questions 166-175

166. lieutenant-governor; 167. 2; 168. counties; 169. Rhode Island;
170. Hawaii; 171. Congress; 172. United States Supreme; 173. Hawaii;
174. the people of the state; 175. Senate.

PHOTO CREDITS